"An insightful and timeless depiction of three past failures that offers present day lessons for managing modern conflicts."

—Jim McDermott, *Bitter Is The Wind*

"Steven Schlesser brings fresh insight to the Battle of the Little Bighorn, the epic 'Titanic' disaster, and the diplomatic failures which led to World War One. His prose is concise and engaging. I read this book straight through and was better for it."

—Terence O'Donnell, *Garden of the Brave in War*

"It is possible to learn as much from a
failed experiment as from a successful one."

—Grant Gilmore
The Death of Contract

The **Soldier,**
The **Builder** &
The **Diplomat**
Steven Schlesser

Studies in Failure
The curious phenomenon of avoidable failure
with hints of its terrible consequences in the
Twentieth and Twenty-First Centuries.

 Cune

The Soldier, the Builder & the Diplomat
© 2023 by Steven Schlesser   All Rights Reserved

Cune Press, Seattle, 2023
ISBN 9781951082260 Paperback
Second Edition

Woodblock prints on cover and interior
© 2005 Jef Gunn, Portland, Oregon.
Cover design © 2022 Adam McIsaak, Portland, Oregon.
Editing by Dan Watkins of verbworks.com

Library of Congress Cataloging-in-Publication Data

Names: Schlesser, Steven, 1957- author.
Title: The soldier, the builder, & the diplomat : studies in failure /
    Steven Schlesser.
Other titles: Soldier, the builder, and the diplomat
Description: Second edition. | Seattle : Cune Press, 2023. | "The curious
    phenomenon of avoidable failure with hints of its terrible consequences
    in the Twentieth Century." | Includes bibliographical references and
    index.
Identifiers: LCCN 2022045405 (print) | LCCN 2022045406 (ebook) | ISBN
    9781951082260 (paperback) | ISBN 9781614574361 (epub)
Subjects: LCSH: History, Modern--19th century. | History, Modern--20th
    century. | Failure (Psychology)--Case studies. | Leadership--Case
    studies. | Custer, George A. (George Armstrong), 1839-1876. | Little
    Bighorn, Battle of the, Mont., 1876. | Andrews, Thomas, 1873-1912. |
    Titanic (Steamship) | Grey of Fallodon, Edward Grey, Viscount,
    1862-1933. | World War, 1914-1918--Diplomatic history.
Classification: LCC D359.7 .S28 2022 (print) | LCC D359.7 (ebook) | DDC
    909.81--dc23/eng/20220923
LC record available at https://lccn.loc.gov/2022045405
LC ebook record available at https://lccn.loc.gov/2022045406

CONTENTS

ILLUSTRATIONS

INTRODUCTION

"Those who cannot remember the past are condemned to repeat it"
—*George Santayana From his work; Life of Reason, Reason in Common Sense, 1905. It should be noted that William Shirer included the quote as an epigraph in his literary work The Rise and Fall of the Third Reich in 1959.*

What does the Battle of the Little Bighorn have to do with the Vietnam War or the intelligence failures of 9/11? What does the sinking of the *RMS Titanic* have to do with the decision to launch the Space Shuttle Challenger or the crash of ValuJet Flight 592? What can the diplomatic failures of 1914 that lead to the Great War teach us?

In the precarious unfolding of history, we can view our occupation and hasty exit from Afghanistan, the Russia-Ukraine War, and the increasingly militant People's Republic of China through the lens of these three events: George Custer's failure at Little Bighorn, the sinking of the *Titanic*, and the breakdown of the world order and WWI. A re-examination of history is more important than ever as we move into a dangerous time of nationalism and warfare.

What lessons can generals and diplomats, builders and businessmen, politicians and scientists gain from a careful examination of the road leading up to a disaster? Unfortunately, the folly of those who ignore the lessons from historical failures persist in example after example: Lyndon Johnson continuing to send more and more troops to Vietnam even though the war was unpopular and clearly unwinnable; George W. Bush invading Iraq in 2003 without a concrete exit strategy, empowering our enemies to engage in asymmetrical warfare and to reveal our vulnerabilities; the Obama administration officials who worked to depose Gaddafi without occupying Libya, unleashing a flood of refugees to storm Europe feeding an environment of xenophobia and the rise of right-wing governments in Poland, Romania, and Bulgaria, the Nazi resurgence in the EU, especially Germany, and the adoption of Brexit in the UK.

In 2014 Barrack Obama and his administration failed in their response to Putin's conquest of Crimea. In late March of 2014 in Brussels, Obama delivered a keynote address as the culmination of his European Tour, rejecting Russia's invasion of Ukraine point by point with Ivy-league logic. Obama failed to mention America's commitment to Ukraine memorialized by the Budapest Agreement signed by President Clinton when we agreed to denude Ukraine of its nuclear weapons.

Moreover, Putin had no time for another tutorial in which Obama underscored his assertion that in the 21st century the borders of Europe cannot be redrawn by force, that international law matters. Yet the Russian President invaded and occupied Crimea in three weeks at zero cost to this own country. Nothing Obama said or did following this land grab gave the Russian leader a compelling reason to rethink his assault on the post-cold war order. In fact, just the opposite: the February 2022 invasion of Ukraine is testimony to our foreign policy failure in this context.

When I began work on this book, I had planned to call it "Edward Grey and the Germans" since my focus back then was how this civilized, decent man, as Britain's Foreign Secretary, struggled to prevent the onset of what turned out to be a barbaric, dehumanizing war that gave birth to a second war thirty years later.

As I wrestled with the subject, I realized that my true interest was narrower. What I really wanted to address was the nature of Edward Grey's failure. I wanted to focus on the idea of failure.

I put away the original plan for my book and thought more about the subject of failure. I realized that a similar phenomenon was embodied in two other events: Custer's defeat at the Battle of the Little Bighorn and the sinking of the *Titanic*. In all three examples, the protagonist was confronted by terrible circumstances—for Custer and Thomas Andrews (builder of the Titanic) these were circumstances of their own making. In each case, in the moment before disaster engulfed them, these three men experienced an historical epiphany—the sudden illumination of permanently changed circumstances of historical significance.

Custer's defeat was, in a small fashion, a product of the US government's inhumane and inconsistent policy towards Native Americans. In the second episode, Thomas Andrews failed to construct a ship that would withstand twelve square feet of damage from an iceberg, a reminder of what can follow from an over-reliance on technology--particularly now when the countries of the world are far more entangled.

Perhaps there is no more notable example of this than the failure of imagination discussed in Chapter Eleven of the *9-11 Commission Report*. One of the principal lessons arising from this report--and how it ties in with Custer, Andrews, and Grey--is to consider historical events carefully to determine what warnings are relevant. In discussing these three events, I hope to give readers a greater sense of discrimination in assessing the quality of the warnings preceding the disaster.

Afghanistan becomes a central subject both because of our failure in our occupation of this small country and in our hurried exit, which may have signaled to Russia that we were not in the position to deliver a firm response to Putin in his aggression towards Ukraine. Of course, in the context of relevant warnings, the Biden Administration had to wrestle with conflicting signals as to how quickly the Afghan government in Kabul might collapse. Well over a month before the August 31 deadline to withdraw troops, an internal State Department memo warned top agency officials of the impending victory of the Taliban.

This state department cable draws parallels to the problems of Group Think I outlined in the Pearl Harbor fiasco as well as the warnings that came to the US government prior to the 9/11 attack. How does one weigh the gravity of warnings? The classified cable represented the clearest evidence yet the Biden Administration had been warned by officials on the ground that the Taliban's advance on Kabul was imminent and that Afghanistan's military might be unable to stop it.

President Trump was equally to blame for starting the poorly reasoned policy of hurried withdrawal and by failing to include officials of the Afghan government in the Doha Accords.

Trump would add insult to injury in his preposterous hold-up to Ukraine of $400 million in military aide that the country desperately needed. In fact, former Trump national security staffer, Lt. Col. Vindman, has stated publicly that Trump's intervention weakened Ukrainian efforts to counteract Russian aggression in a number of ways.

Of course, I have written this book with the privilege of hindsight--a benefit that the 9/11 commissioners also found to be a handicap to their analysis. They wrote that the warnings leading up to 9/11 were so salient they were concerned about missing the nuances of smaller details.

In other words, the official who is to decide the course of an action must first sort out what signals are relevant and leave behind those which are irrelevant. Then the official must incorporate his discrimination (informed by his own personal history) to determine the importance of those relevant signals. He must, as it were, place them into a hierarchy. In addition to this, he must believe that a particular danger is compelling. Captain Smith of the *Titanic* failed this first threshold. He did not believe that an upcoming ice field in the North Atlantic represented a serious threat to his ship.

How do you teach imagination? Custer certainly had the experience to appreciate the potential dangers of attacking an Indian village filled with hostile Sioux and Cheyenne warriors, but he did not have the imagination to foresee just how many warriors would counterattack or that their motivation would be so deadly. Thomas Andrews was fully aware that he could design a ship with more enhanced safety features than he implemented into the Titanic, but he never imagined that his ship might strike a rock, another ship, or an iceberg that would puncture the hull at points beyond the junction of two watertight compartments. Edward Grey, on the other hand, could imagine the terrible loss of life that would result from a general European war, but he lacked the imagination to foresee that his policy of balancing European powers against one another might set into motion a chain reaction of warring countries.

This book sets out the circumstances and highlights the point where the lack of imagination in these three events overtake them and doom them to catastrophic and history-making failure.

(Preceding page: General George Armstrong Custer.)

THE STRANGE RIDE
OF GEORGE CUSTER

I

THE DRAMA BEGAN ON THE DRY SLOPES of the American plains with George Armstrong Custer washing his hands at the confluence of the Yellowstone and Rosebud Rivers on June 21, 1876. Custer stood knee-deep in the river, holding a pewter basin with a bar of soap bobbing in it. The morning was unusually cold and several of Custer's men along the riverbank viewed their leader with curiosity. Throughout his career, Custer washed his hands as often as eight or nine times a day, even in cold weather. In addition, this thirty-seven-year-old cavalry leader slicked his hair down with cinnamon oil and brushed his teeth with salt. Custer had always been sensitive about his personal appearance. He was handsome. Photographs reveal soft northern features—freckles, high cheekbones, bright, sensitive eyes—quite unlike artistic depictions of him as a fierce, Teutonic warrior. Custer's face, innocent and childlike, was in sharp contrast to his deeds.

Later that day, Custer was summoned to the command steamer, *Far West*, anchored in the Yellowstone River. This boat was 190 feet long with a beam of nearly thirty-five feet. She bore two steam capstans designed to help negotiate rapids and other shallow places in these western rivers. A boatman rowed Custer out to the vessel and, after climbing aboard deck, he presented himself to his commanding officers, General Alfred Terry and Colonel John Gibbon. The three men sat at a table inside the large cabin—normally this cabin could hold thirty passengers comfortably—and reviewed a map spread out before them. From the reports of their scouts,

Terry and Gibbon told Custer that they believed Sitting Bull's band of Sioux Indians was camped somewhere up the Rosebud River or perhaps in the Little Bighorn Valley. Since this group of Indians had refused to come to a reservation, and because of their consistent attacks upon white settlers, they were considered "hostile," as opposed to the Indian tribes who had been cooperative with the whites. After some discussion, Terry told Custer that he would issue written orders that would send his Seventh Cavalry on the hunt first, heading down the Rosebud Valley, and then swinging west toward the Little Bighorn. Custer was to make sure the Indians did not escape to the south or the east.

After the meeting, Custer embarked on preparations. He arranged for his stag hounds to be left with the wagons. He transferred his brother, Boston Custer, and his nephew, Autie Reed, from the quartermaster's department so they could accompany him. He told his senior officers to prepare their men with the proper supplies. From a trading post, the soldiers could buy tobacco, and shirts more comfortable than what the army provided, and straw hats for the midday heat. Ironically, these were goods intended for the Indians, and purloined by federal government Indian agents before they could be delivered. That evening, Custer joined some of his men for a poker game on board the steamer. During a break in the game, Major James S. Brisbin, Gibbon's second-in-command, found Custer outside on one of the forward decks. Custer told Brisbin he had decided against taking Gatling guns since their weight and awkwardness might impede his progress.

The next day, June 22, Custer led over seven hundred men of his Seventh Cavalry in a parade before Gibbon and Terry as a suitable preface to his forthcoming campaign. The circumstance of this brash, headstrong man riding toward a village inhabited by thousands of Indians was emblematic of the federal government's policy toward the aboriginal people of America.

In 1868, the United States government had arranged a treaty with the Sioux Indians, setting apart for them a huge tract of land comprising the western half of what is now South Dakota. The government intended to reserve this area for the Sioux "for all time," but six years later Custer led an expedition that found gold in the Black Hills. Gold meant prospectors. Prospectors meant an on-rush of whites, mostly families and merchants. In addition, railroad executives began to push for an east-to-west line through the area. Clashes between whites and Sioux followed. Often these clashes took the form of Indian attacks upon wagons of whites moving west or upon prospectors who had strayed beyond what experienced Indian fighters considered "safe" territory.

Often the Indians would leave these prospectors riddled with arrows or mutilated as a warning to other white men who might intrude into their territory. Toward the close of 1875, this Sioux belligerency alarmed the government's Indian Department which, in turn, nudged the government's War Department to take action. The commander in the West, General Phil Sheridan, a short, Irish-American Civil War general, drew up plans to deal with the Indian problem. Sheridan conferred with his boss, General William Sherman, who considered winter the best time to operate against the Indians. Sherman gave Sheridan the authority to design a plan of attack that called for three columns of troops to march against the hostile Sioux and Cheyennes. One column would be commanded by General George Crook, an experienced Indian fighter and decorated Civil War veteran.

Crook's column would advance from Fort Fetterman in Wyoming northward into the Powder River country. A second column would be commanded by Colonel Gibbon eastward from the Montana forts along the Yellowstone River. The third column, to be known as the "Dakota column," was commanded by General Terry and would move west from Fort Abraham Lincoln, following the course of the Yellowstone.

Sheridan expected these three columns to rendezvous at a common center, probably near the Bighorn or the Little Bighorn Rivers, although as James Welch points out in his excellent history, *Killing Custer: The Battle of the Little Bighorn and The Fate of the Plains Indians*, this expected rendezvous between the three columns was wishful thinking at best, given the poor state of frontier communications and given that Terry and Gibbon had no idea of Crook's actual whereabouts. "The likelihood that all three columns would come together at once was remote," wrote Welch, "especially since the planners did not know exactly where the Indians were. It is almost astonishing that the plan worked as well as it did, in that all three battalions had some contact with the Indians."

II

ON THIS DAY, JUNE 22, WITHIN TWO WEEKS of the country's official centennial celebration, Terry reiterated his order that Custer scout the area for Indians along the Rosebud River Valley. Custer was supposed to wait somewhere along the Little Bighorn River for Gibbon's column, in combination with Terry's remaining companies, to march down the Bighorn

River to meet four days later for battle. Unfortunately, Terry's written instructions to Custer were vague on one critical point: What was Custer to do if he found the Indian camp first?

Examining Custer's past behavior, one discovers a simple answer: charge! In fact, Custer had been charging into battles all his life and was lucky at this point not to have been killed. Several times during the Civil War, in similar charges against Confederate soldiers, Custer's horse had been shot out from under him. Unlike a textbook commander seated dispassionately inside his command tent, Custer rode at the head of his troops each time he made the decision to attack the enemy.

Today, Custer wore a tan buckskin suit and a white, flat-topped hat characteristic of the Plains. In the Nineteenth Century, the United States Army was not as rigid about military dress code as it is now and Custer took full advantage. During the Civil War, Custer had donned the uniforms of at least one of his captured opponents. He often wore striped pants and colorful neck attire. One of his contemporaries described him as giving the impression of a ringleader at a circus.

In spite of his dandyism, Custer took his job as a military officer of the United States Army seriously. At times, too seriously. His commanding officers counseled restraint. The last order Custer would ever receive—more of a suggestion than an order—came from Colonel Gibbon as Custer prepared to follow the troopers of the Seventh Cavalry as they rode out of the camp. "Now, Custer, don't be greedy," said Gibbon. "Wait for us."

"Custer, don't be greedy." What a futile admonition! Aside from his natural inclination for immediate engagement, Custer had other reasons for ignoring Gibbon's advice. He harbored ambitions to be a presidential candidate on the Democratic ticket. Once he told a group of Indian scouts, "When we return, I will go back to Washington, and on my trip to Washington I shall take my brother here, Bloody Knife, with me. I shall remain at Washington and be the Great Father." Moreover, Custer calculated that a quick victory over these hostile Indians would accomplish two goals. First, defeating the Indians by the twenty-sixth of June would allow Custer enough time to return to camp, board the nearest eastbound train, and appear at the centennial celebration in Philadelphia on the Fourth of July. Second, a victory engineered solely by Custer would give him the necessary notoriety for a shot at the presidency. Custer must have assumed that the American people, or American politicians, would hold him in a favorable light for single-handedly engineering a massacre of an Indian village. But the country was divided on the question of dealing with Indians. Many of Custer's countrymen, particularly those from the East, felt that persecuting Indians in the West was unbecoming, particularly because four years of their lives and industry had been spent fighting to free the slaves. Moreover, a healthy debate in the country raged following the Chivington or Sand Creek Massacre of November 29, 1864. Colonel John Chivington, a former Methodist minister and Civil War fighter, threw six hundred bloodthirsty soldiers against two hundred Indian warriors and five hundred women and children. The slaughter was appalling. Suddenly, the American West of the Nineteenth Century began to resemble Eastern Europe seventy-five years later.

III

CUSTER, THE GOOD SOLDIER, COULD KILL QUITE EASILY. During the Civil War, in the summer of 1862, Custer gave chase to a mounted Confederate officer after Custer's regiment broke the enemy position at White Oak Swamp. The Confederate officer jumped a rail fence. Custer stayed right on his heels and later wrote proudly to his sister, "I selected him as my game." Custer yelled at the officer to surrender, but the chase continued. Custer fired his weapon and missed. He fired a second time. The Confederate straightened and then fell to the ground. A witness said the enemy officer managed to get to his feet and hold up both hands before he collapsed, dying with blood gushing from his mouth.

A characteristic photograph of Custer taken at Fort Lincoln before the 1876 campaign against the Sioux depicts him in his living room, writing. In the photograph, mounted animal heads adorn the walls. Perhaps Custer was writing an article for *Galaxy*, the magazine that had published installments of his autobiography, *My Life on the Plains*, from January 1872 to October 1874.

In his autobiography, Custer saw himself as a solitary man holding aloft the torch of civilization—Western civilization, white civilization. He wrote, "Stripped of the beautiful romance with which we have been so long willing to envelop him, transferred from the inviting pages of the novelist to the localities where we are compelled to meet with him, in his native village, on the war path, and when raiding upon our frontier settlements and lines of travel, the Indian forfeits his claim to the appellation of the *noble* red man. We see him as he is, and, so far as all knowledge goes, as he ever has been, a *savage* in every sense of the word."

Custer's thesis was that war imposed civilization. In his book, *Cra-*

zy Horse and Custer: Two American Warriors, Stephen Ambrose contrasts Custer's view of civilization with the ideas of Crazy Horse. Custer believed in the traditional Western view that man's purpose under God was to improve himself and his society, particularly in a material sense. Unlike Crazy Horse, who lived for the present, Custer acted with his eyes on the future: one more Civil War victory to propel him to a higher rank; one more successful Indian battle to vault him to high political office. Restless and driven, Custer tied cause and effect to a sequence of military victories. In this way, Custer was a child of Western European tradition. And he saw the conquest of the American West as an opportunity for white settlement that would bring a clearing of the land, small farms, and saw mills. In other words, the farmers and yeomen who had descended from Europeans would replace the uncivilized hunter-gatherers who were then inhabiting the American West.

IV

ON JUNE 22, 1876, CUSTER LED A PACK OF SOLDIERS toward Crazy Horse, Sitting Bull, and the other Indians living free on the land. Custer marched his men twelve miles, then made camp at the foot of a steep bluff with enough grass and deadwood for campfires. At sunset, the officers of the Seventh Cavalry assembled at Custer's tent for a somewhat awkward conference in which Custer outlined his plans and justified his actions.

At the head of the Seventh, Custer was supported—or perhaps plagued— by his two principal subordinates: Major Marcus Reno and Captain Frederick Benteen. Reno was a dark-featured, stocky man who graduated from West Point in the class of 1857 (four years before Custer). Like his commanding officer, Reno acquired numerous demerits; he finished twentieth in a class of thirty-eight, but better than Custer, who finished dead last. Benteen, on the other hand, came from the South and, against his father's wishes, chose to fight on the side of the Union. Prematurely gray and baby-faced, Benteen irritated Custer by questioning his orders and his leadership abilities.

Assembling Reno and Benteen, along with the other subordinate officers of the Seventh, Custer discussed the scouting mission upon which Reno had embarked days earlier. It was Major Reno, in fact, who with a small party had discovered the trail of the Indians that Custer was now chasing. From the information in Reno's report, Custer did not expect to encounter more than a thousand warriors. Confident in the fighting abilities of his Seventh Cavalry, he had refused the offer of additional men.

According to one participant of this conference, Edward S. Godfrey, whose account of the battle appeared in an 1892 edition of *Century Magazine*, Custer appeared ill at ease. "This 'talk' of his, as we called it, was considered at the time as something extra ordinary for General Custer, for it was not his habit to unbosom himself to his officers. In it he showed concessions and a reliance on others; there was an indefinable something that was *not* Custer. His manner and tone, usually brusque and aggressive or somewhat curt, was on this occasion conciliating and subdued. There was something akin to an appeal, as if depressed, that made a deep impression on all present. We compared watches to get the official time, and separated to attend to our various duties. Lieutenants McIntosh, Wallace (later killed at the Battle of Wounded Knee, December 29, 1890), and myself walked to our bivouac, for some distance in silence, when Wallace remarked: 'Godfrey, I believe General Custer is going to be killed.' 'Why? Wallace,' I replied, 'what makes you think so?' 'Because,' said he, 'I have never heard Custer talk in that way before.'"

During the conference, Custer had mentioned that, in trying to determine the number of hostile Indians ahead, he had "consulted the reports of the Commissioner of Indian Affairs"—a curious bit of homework at best, given that the federal government's "Indian people" not only possessed little useful information, but also helped to get the Seventh Cavalry into this soup in the first place.

V

THIS SAD STORY BEGAN AFTER THE CIVIL WAR, in 1865, when the federal government had the opportunity to look westward. Before then, the United States Indian policy had been an accumulation of seventy years of broken treaties, intermittent warfare, and blatant inconsistencies. Now, the Civil War heroes of the victorious North turned their attention to the Indians in the West, and did so under the watchful eyes of an American public who had become sensitive to Indian concerns, particularly after the Sand Creek Massacre of November 1864. Moreover, military action was not necessarily considered the answer. By the end of 1865, President Andrew Johnson noted, with sharp disapproval, the excessive costs of the Western campaign in which army columns encountered only scattered tribes but rang up twenty million dollars in invoices.

Nevertheless, the government's chief army man, General William T.

Sherman, argued strenuously that the white Americans migrating west needed protection from the Indians, particularly along the major trails. To protect these emigrants, Sherman organized what he described as points of rendezvous for his troops at Forts Ridgley, Abercrombie, Kearny, Riley, and Larned. This scheme had mixed success. Sherman then went a step further. At the end of 1866, he developed a comprehensive plan to restrict the Sioux to an area north of the Platte, west of the Missouri, and east of the Bozeman Trail. In addition, the Arapaho, Cheyenne, Comanche, Kiowa, Apache, and Navajo Indian tribes would be kept south of the Arkansas and east of Fort Union, New Mexico. Such a plan, in which Indians were told by their white masters where to live, foreshadows how the Nazis resettled Jews into ghettos in Warsaw, Lodz, and other sites in Eastern Europe.

On December 21, 1866, a brash army officer named William Fetterman rushed from Fort Kearny with eighty soldiers in pursuit of a party of Sioux. The Sioux drew Fetterman and his men into a classic ambush and killed every last one of them. The massacre shocked the nation. Sherman, then commanding the Division of Missouri, wrote a letter to his subordinate, General Phillip St. George Cooke, that the Fetterman incident should be treated as an act of war and that the United States Army should kill ten Indians for every white man who lost his life.

During those cold, closed-in days of early 1867, little was accomplished. A spring offensive—against an enemy clever enough to fight only when it suited them—proved fruitless and expensive. Congress formed a Peace Commission to deal with the Indian problem. Included as commissioners were Sherman, Brigadier General Terry (later Custer's boss), and General William Harney, a career Indian fighter. Pressure from Washington to make peace with the Indians spurred the Peace Commission to fashion the Sioux Treaty of 1868 that said the Sioux could live permanently in the portion of South Dakota west of the Missouri River, a territory that included the Black Hills. In addition, the Sioux were granted hunting rights in the Powder River country that stretched from the Black Hills to the Bighorn Mountains, an area whites were not permitted to enter. No changes could be made to the treaty without the consent of three-quarters of the adult male Sioux population. The United States government would provide supplies to the Sioux while they adjusted to these boundaries.

Problems with this treaty arose immediately. The concept of boundaries did not register with many Sioux, so they proceeded to hunt outside of the reservation. One major difficulty for the Indians was the government's failure to consider the buffalo hunts as the Sioux's principal way of life.

26

Government agencies were set up along the Missouri River on the eastern edge of the reservation, a long way from the buffalo herds. The Washington peace people expected Indians to farm, but many refused to do so and those who tried found the land intractable. For those whites in the West—and particularly for the military men—this was, as Sherman put it, more of a truce than a peace treaty. However one describes it, the treaty and its resulting machinations were bad government policy.

The US Army's plan was to drive the Indians onto reservations north of the Platte River. The policy, critical Easterners alleged, was to bribe the Indians with guns and ammunition once they arrived at the reservations. Legally, they were under the jurisdiction of the Bureau of Indian Affairs which was controlled by the Department of the Interior. The Bureau sent its agents into the field and received reports back that the Indians were docile and compliant. Members of the army maintained that the agents lied and then compounded their lies by selling arms and ammunition to the Indians. Custer's two immediate subordinate officers knew that much of the Indian "problem" stemmed from the inconsistencies of the US government. Captain Benteen later said that the principal cause of Indian unrest was the enormous pilfering done by the Indian agents, some of whom managed to pocket thirteen to fifteen thousand dollars above and beyond an annual salary a tenth of that. Reno put it more bluntly: What kind of government asks its soldiers to fight an enemy that the government has already supplied with arms?

Custer was not concerned with shades of meaning or veiled intentions within the bureaucracies of the United States government. His concern was making war on hostile Indians. The morning after he staged his informal conference with his officers in his tent, he rose early, well before five. As he began his march at the head of the column, two sergeants followed immediately behind. One bore the regimental standard, the other carried Custer's personal standard—the same one he used while commanding a cavalry division in the Civil War. Along the way, scouts found traces of Indian wickiups—huts covered with brushwood, inside of which Indians would spread blankets for temporary shelter. Around the perimeter of this temporary camp, the scouts found even more disturbing signs. The grass had been eaten down to short stubs for miles around. There were enough horse droppings to indicate not just several hundred horses but thousands. As the column covered another fifteen miles, they discovered signs of more Indian camps and a converging trail that the scouts felt came from a large body of Indians—Sioux, Cheyennes, and Arapahoes—that had left the reservations and holding areas to join Sitting Bull.

The ground was rough. Little grass remained for the cavalry horses. Custer halted his men around five that afternoon on the right bank of the Rosebud at the mouth of Beaver Creek where finally they were able to find some grass for the horses. They had come thirty-three miles and this group—officially a scouting party for Terry and Gibbon—was closing in on a large assembly of Indians. Once Custer found these Indians, his first option was to wait for reinforcements. But that was not likely. Earlier on this day, he told his scouts, "Here's where Reno made the mistake of his life," referring to Reno's early stumble onto the trail of all these Indians. "He had six troops of cavalry and rations enough for a number of days. He'd have made a name for himself if he'd pushed on after them."

VI

CUSTER HAD ALREADY MADE A NAME FOR HIMSELF by doing just that. In September of 1868, he was asked by his immediate superior, General Sheridan, to launch a winter campaign against hostile Indians—this time the Southern Cheyennes in Oklahoma.

Sheridan and his boss, Sherman, had decided to punish any Indians who raided white settlements or military posts. The US military—unlike some peace-minded civilians in Washington, DC—would deal with these hostile Indians with the same total war approach used by Sherman against Southerners in the Civil War. A letter from Sherman to Sheridan dated October 15, 1868, reads, "Go ahead in your own way and I will back you with my whole authority. If it results in the utter annihilation of these Indians, it is but the result of what they have been warned of again and again. . . . I will say nothing and do nothing to restrain our troops from doing what they deem proper on the spot and will allow no mere vague general charges of cruelty and inhumanity to tie their hands, but will use all the powers confided to me to the end that these Indians, the enemies of our race and of our civilization, shall not again be able to begin and carry out their barbarous warfare on any kind of pretext they may choose to allege."

Sheridan had decided to mount a winter campaign against the Cheyennes because they were so difficult to engage in direct combat during the summer. Summoned by Sheridan from his home in Michigan, Custer eagerly accepted his duties, leading a mixed force of infantry and cavalry to the North Canadian River near the Oklahoma panhandle, where they built Camp Supply just south of the Kansas border.

On November 23, 1868, Custer set off with his men through the snow to track the Indians. After three days of marching, he discovered the trail of Indians returning from Kansas to their village in Oklahoma. Along with the help of his Osage guides, he found what he was looking for—a camp of Cheyennes along the Washita River. The cry of a child in the night identified this collection of Indians. Although Custer did not then know it, this camp was headed by Black Kettle, the same chief who had suffered through the earlier attack near Sand Creek at the hands of Chivington.

Custer retired from his viewpoint of the village to his collection of officers and ordered them to split the column into four detachments. Each detachment would attack the village from a separate side. Once each was in place, Custer would give the signal to attack shortly after dawn. But, having failed to do an adequate reconnaissance of the village, Custer had little idea as to the number of warriors he would face. In addition, he was splitting his forces—a risky endeavor at best—and he had no adequate supplies or backup should the battle last longer than the initial engagements. Nevertheless, Custer was in his element.

When dawn came, he instructed his band to play the Irish drinking song, "Gary Owen," which signalled a four-pronged charge into the sleeping Indian village, firing through the teepees. Dazed warriors emerged. Custer and his men shot anything that moved. Several of the Indians took cover along the bank of the Washita, but Custer's men so overwhelmed the village with the first assault that resistance was minimal.

Moreover, Custer's killing was indiscriminate. He and his troops shot squaws, children, and old men. One of his officers, Major Elliott, took a company of men and chased some escaping warriors down the river. Later Custer would be blamed for not retrieving his soldiers (Elliott and his men were killed). But, in the meantime, Custer had other things to do. He ordered the village burned, including over a thousand buffalo robes, ceremonial clothing, seven hundred pounds of tobacco, and several tons of meat. He told the Indian prisoners who had survived the fight—the squaws and their children who had been hiding—to select ponies from the Indian herd for the ride back and then instructed the men to kill the remaining eight hundred ponies.

Once Custer was finished with all this butchery in the snow, the village looked, in the words of a New York newspaper, like "a slaughter pen." Like the My Lai Massacre in the Vietnam War, the corpses of men, women, and children, smeared with mud, were piled up on top of one another in ditches and holes. Sheridan had a tidy answer for the slaughter of noncombatants.

"If a village is attacked and women and children are killed the responsibility is not with the soldiers but with the people whose crime necessitated the attack. During the war did any one hesitate to attack a village or town occupied by the enemy because women or children were within its limits? Did we cease to throw shells into Vicksburg or Atlanta because women and children were there?"

The Battle of Washita is significant for several reasons. First, Custer had a smashing military success against Indians that brought him more fame and bolstered his confidence. Second, Custer achieved this victory without proper reconnaissance. Third, Custer split his forces and was successful. Now, on the morning of June 24, 1876, two days after leaving General Terry on this scouting mission to find hostile Indians, Custer looked across the landscape of the Rosebud Valley and knew once again he was close to his enemy. He had his troops on the march early in the morning, although progress was slower this day because the column had to wait behind the Crow scouts who worked to keep on the Indian trail. Signs of a large population of Indians were growing. Markings from pony herds and lodge poles indicated that many tribes had converged in the area. The weather was hot and dry. The troops were forced to march on separate trails because so much dust was kicked up into the air. Toward dusk, Custer ordered his group to halt near the cover of a bluff.

Finally, his men had a chance to rest. This was a pristine place. The Rosebud River lay three hundred yards to the east and, in between, thickets of wild rose bushes were in bloom. The men ate their dinner. Afterwards, they were ordered to extinguish their campfires. Now, at 9:30 PM, the officers of the Seventh Cavalry expected to sleep, but returning Crow scouts reported that a large group of hostiles had crossed from the Rosebud Valley toward the valley of the Little Bighorn. Custer assembled his officers in the candlelight of his bivouac and explained that he was ordering a night march to bring the Seventh Cavalry close to the divide between the two valleys by morning. This would give him time, he explained, to study the country throughout the day of the twenty-fifth, locate the village, and prepare to attack the next morning.

A night march through that country was difficult. Essentially, the men had to follow the dust rising ahead of them and then, when that was not sufficient, they had to stop and listen carefully to the sounds of horses up ahead. Custer halted his men again at 2:00 AM. They rested. Then, sometime before eight in the morning, news came that the scouts had located an immense Indian village, twelve or fifteen miles beyond the divide in the valley of the Little Bighorn. Now tensions rose. The Crow scouts met with Custer and told him an attack would be a disaster. His chief scout and friend, Bloody Knife, said that there were enough Indians in the valley to keep a fight alive for two or three days, to which Custer replied, "I guess we'll get through with them in one day."

This curious bit of bravado reveals not so much foolhardiness as it does Custer's own personal history. He had always succeeded in military endeavors by attacking first. Attack. Attack. Attack. And yet, this time, all the signs were bad. First, his scouts kept reiterating that the Indian village might have as many as two thousand warriors. Second, he had pushed his men hard, and even though they were exhausted, he intended to continue to march them. Third, the Indians below (and Custer of course did not know this) had every reason in the world to fight with fearsome aggressiveness. Already a column of General Crook's had engaged these same hostiles and had been forced to retreat. Finally, these Indians were enjoying a last season of freedom. Since they had agreed to the terms of the Sioux Treaty of 1868, the Indians discovered the whites violating its provisions again and again, none more egregious than the expedition into the Black Hills in 1874.

VII

CUSTER HAD BEEN INVOLVED IN THE BLACK HILLS events as well. At the time, the country was in desperate financial shape and President Ulysses S. Grant had needed some event to distract the American public. Grant conferred with Sheridan, commander of the Department of the Missouri, and together they decided upon a military and scientific expedition into the Black Hills of South Dakota, an area ceded to the Indians in the treaty of 1868.

Although the expedition was clearly a treaty violation, Sheridan nevertheless justified it by declaring that the Indians had violated the treaty by killing settlers in Nebraska and by hampering construction of the Northern Pacific Railroad. Sheridan summoned Custer to lead the expedition, a task on which he embarked with enthusiasm. The Indians whose land Custer would violate dubbed Custer's route the "thieves trail" and Custer the "chief of thieves."

This was not the first time that Custer trooped into Indian territory. In 1873, along with Colonel David S. Stanley, Custer had led the Seventh Cavalry to the Yellowstone River to provide protection for surveyors of the

Northern Pacific Railroad. But the Black Hills trip outraged the Indians, because the scientific inquiry was really a veiled investigation into the amount of gold that lay in the area. The trip was a huge success for Grant and his administration. Custer had found lots of gold—the press on the East Coast dubbed it a new gold rush—and suddenly a depressed country had hope.

VIII

NOW, ON THE MORNING OF JUNE 25, 1876, Custer was set once again to provide white Americans with a dose of good news. As he had at the Battle of Washita, Custer sought to fulfill his superiors' expectations: a decisive military victory over hostile Indians. And, yet, even at this point—8:00 AM on June 25—Custer had no idea of the size of the group he would face.

Earlier, Custer's scouts had determined that the Indians had settled about the Little Bighorn Valley. Lieutenant Charles Varnum, Mitch Bouyer, and other scouts had been sent ahead of the rest of the column to discover their exact whereabouts. The scouts reached a rocky promontory called the Crow's Nest about three o'clock in the morning. Varnum took a nap while the others waited for dawn. Soon, in the clear, they saw unmistakable signs of a massive village. Hundreds and hundreds of white lodges dotted the landscape in the valley below. The scouts could also see an enormous pony herd. Varnum sent two of the scouts back to camp to inform Custer that they had located the village. After they had left, Varnum and his men spotted several enemy Indians on horseback about a mile-and-a-half to the west. Some time later they saw more hostiles to the northeast. This caused Varnum to worry that the Indian leaders in the village would soon know how close Custer actually was to them.

That morning, as these reports arrived back to the Seventh Cavalry, Custer was likely debating in his own mind the prospects of attacking the Indian village that very day. Certainly, General Terry gave Custer enough leeway either to attack or to remain vigilant and wait for reinforcements. The original plan—as Sheridan conceived it—was that this group of Indians should feel the blows of a three-pronged pincer movement. However, because of poor communication between the military groups, Terry had no idea of the whereabouts of Crook's column. Gibbon's column was to proceed to the mouth of the Big Horn River and then follow up the fork of the Little Bighorn, trapping the Indians. Terry's written instructions to Custer were, unfortunately, vague on the critical point of what Custer should do once he found the Indians. Terry's instructions to Custer:

(Sitting Bull.)

Camp at the Mouth of the Rosebud River: June 22, 1876. To Lt. Colonel Custer, 7th Cavalry. Colonel: The Brigadier-General commanding directs that as soon as your regiment can be made ready for the march, you proceed up the Rosebud in pursuit of the Indians whose trail was discovered by Major Reno a few days ago. It is, of course, impossible to give you any definite instructions in regard to this movement, and were it not impossible to do so, the Department Commander places too much confidence in your zeal, energy, and ability to impose upon you precise orders which might hamper your action when nearly in contact with the enemy.

Notice how Terry made no specific mention about cooperating directly with Gibbon's column in this two-pronged attack on the Indians. Even if Terry had been specific—that Custer was to find the Indians first and then wait for Gibbon to be in position—Gibbon was too slow, hampered as he was by the infantry, and he had a longer line to march than Custer. If the two-pronged attack was to have a real chance, Terry should have set Gibbon on his march much sooner and kept Custer back. Or, he should have been very specific on the point of Custer waiting for Gibbon to be in place before attacking the Indians.

As stated earlier, the whole campaign was prompted by Custer's previous discovery of gold in the Black Hills. President Grant, who had tried and failed to buy the Black Hills from the Indians, sought to turn the country's attention away from the bleak economic conditions in the east with the distraction of an Indian war out west. Opportunities for white settlement would, of course, follow.

The Indians, in their turn, saw the continuing violations of the 1868 treaty as their justification to continue to attack white travelers and white settlements. The wild bands of Sioux Indians who inhabited the Powder River country had no desire to conform to the dictates of the whites. Sitting Bull and Crazy Horse understood the white men well enough to know that their freedom was essentially gone, but they wanted at least one or two more seasons of traveling and living the way they always had. Custer himself noted that, had he been an Indian, he would certainly have put his lot with the hostile Sioux riding free and unburdened along the Plains. As

Edgar Stewart wrote in his book, *Custer's Luck,* "The President of the United States agreed that the discovery of gold and the intrusion of settlers had not caused the war but only complicated it by the uncertainty of the numbers to be encountered. Rather, the issue furnished an excuse for both sides to bring an end to the uncertain and poorly observed truce that had prevailed for seven years. It was almost the universal consensus that only a few hundred warriors at most would dare to oppose the troops and that these could be rounded up in a short campaign, before the grass was up in the spring, as someone expressed it. The peace policy of loving the Indians into submission had failed; the advocates of a more 'realistic' policy were to be given the opportunity to see what they could accomplish with a club."

This club took the form of Sheridan's insistence to Washington that immediate military action against the Sioux was necessary. However, before the army could proceed, the secretary of the interior, Zachariah Chandler, told the commissioner of Indian affairs to order the various Indian agents in Sioux and Cheyenne country to notify the Indians living in their territory to report to the agencies before January 31. The exact language ran as follows: "Referring to our communication of the 27th relative to the status of certain Sioux Indians residing without the bounds of their reservation and their continued hostile attitude toward the whites, I have to request that you direct the Indian agents at all Sioux agencies in Dakota and at Fort Peck Montana to notify said Indians that unless they shall remove within the bounds of their reservation (and remain by) before the 31st January next, they shall be deemed hostile and treated accordingly by the military forces."

January 31, 1876, was the critical date. Many of the Indian chiefs, including Sitting Bull, claimed that they never received this order, though, even if they had, it is doubtful they would have brought their tribes back to the agencies. These Indians felt they had a right to be where they were and that no one had the right to order them onto reservations. At any rate, none of the government officials expected the hostile Indians to comply with the order. Rather, the January 31 ultimatum was more of an excuse to shift the problem away from the peacemakers to the war makers.

IX

CERTAINLY, THIS WOULD NOT BE THE LAST TIME the US government had allowed hardened military men to significantly influence US policy. In early 1964, the war hawks of the Johnson Administration were looking to escalate the Vietnam War. The Joint Chiefs prefaced their plan with an inflated version of the domino theory. South Vietnam was pivotal to America's global confrontation with Communism, went the argument, and a defeat there would deal a blow to the reputation of the United States throughout Asia as well as harm America's image in Africa and Latin America.

Johnson subscribed to the adage that "wars are too serious to be entrusted to generals." But he also feared the Pentagon lobbyists. He knew that the Pentagon people could persuade conservatives in Congress to sabotage his social legislation unless he satisfied their demands. As he prepared himself for the 1964 campaign, he was especially sensitive to those who might brand him soft on Communism. He therefore made promises he may never have intended to keep. At a White House reception on Christmas Eve, 1963, for example, he allegedly told the Joint Chiefs of Staff, "Just let me get elected, and then you can have your war." Robert McNamara contends Johnson never said this, but the implication, in our view, was always there.

The next day, Johnson announced his decision to add forty-four American combat battalions to the relatively small US contingents already there. This was a hard decision for Johnson. He had agonized over it during his critical months in the White House, but eventually this was his final judgment. As he would later explain, "There are many, many people who can recommend and advise, and a few of them consent. But there is only one who has been chosen by the American people to decide."

Once Johnson had made this decision he followed through with the Gulf of Tonkin Resolution—a pivotal event in American history in which the Johnson Administration received support from Congress on its Vietnam policy based on an alleged incident between American forces and a North Vietnamese gunboat.

After the Gulf of Tonkin Resolution passed, Lyndon Johnson pursued a vain effort to win the Vietnam War. Clearly, the ensuing military effort was a mistake. And yet the roots of our Vietnam period lay in how we—as Americans—viewed the world and our role in it. In the introduction to his book, *Vietnam: A History*, Stanley Karnow illuminates America's failure in Vietnam. "Looking back, US political and military specialists have diagnosed the struggle in detail, so that studies of the war have become a minor industry. But prescriptions for how America might have averted its defeat in Vietnam are as numerous and as diverse as the analysts. General William C. Westmoreland, who commanded the US forces in Vietnam from 1965 to 1968, predictably claimed in his memoirs that restraints had thwarted his effectiveness. He faulted President Johnson for escalating the war too slowly, refusing to permit incursion against enemy bases in Laos and Cambodia, furnishing the South Vietnamese army with inadequate equipment, and among other things, 'failing to level' with the US public." Other army officers faulted Johnson, as well, because they felt he refused to put the country on a war footing out of fear that a full-scale war would doom his domestic economic and social programs. As a result, they felt they were denied victory. Karnow said that many authorities have even argued that the Joint Chiefs of Staff ought to have resigned rather than accept the limitations enforced on the soldiers in the field.

Unfortunately, the war hawks within the Johnson Administration did not intend to back down from a fight, even if the odds were against them, and they were impatient to carry on a campaign that they felt they could win.

X

THE US MILITARY OF THE NINETEENTH CENTURY acted with equal stubbornness. After the ultimatum date of January 31, 1876, passed without hostile Indians reporting back to their reservations, Secretary of the Interior Chandler notified Secretary of War William Belknap that, "said Indians are hereby turned over to the War Department for such action on the part of the Army as you may deem proper under the circumstances." This bland advice unleashed a War Department who wanted to strike the Indians quickly.

Sherman, with memories of the Sand Creek and Washita battles fresh in his mind, noted that the middle of the winter was the best time to fight Indians. Sheridan agreed with him—winter was the best time to catch, and engage, hostile Indians—and he therefore drafted his famous three-column attack. General Crook would command the southern column heading north out of Fort Fetterman. Colonel Gibbon would command the western column heading east from Fort Shaw. And Custer, as the plan was originally concocted, would command the Dakota column heading west from Fort Lincoln. However, the plan was changed because Custer himself became embroiled in a political controversy.

That controversy, known as the Belknap Affair, was politically motivated. In February of 1876, the *New York Herald* reported that Secretary of War Belknap was "farming out" traderships in the Indian country and that Orvil Grant, the President's brother, was involved as a trader himself. Here is how the scheme worked: Orvil Grant made arrangements with other Indian traders to deliver supplies to them as part of the government's treaty obligations to the Indians. These supplies were shipped up the Missouri River by steamboat, checked out to the recipients but never delivered, and then taken farther up the river and turned over to the post traders. These post traders were paid to receive and then sell these supplies to white settlers. Much of the profits from those sales were split between Orvil Grant and Belknap's wife. A zealous congressman named Hester Clymer formed a committee to investigate this and other abuses in a War Department headed by Belknap.

Always outspoken, Custer made clear his opposition to corruption, bribery, and other abuses by the government in the West, and Clymer summoned him to Washington to testify. Custer at first refused, asking instead that any questions be forwarded to him at Fort Lincoln where he was waiting for the weather to improve to start his troops on Sheridan's march against the Indians. Clymer insisted on a personal appearance. An election was approaching and the Democrats wanted to embarrass President Grant as much as possible. Custer arrived in Washington and delivered extensive testimony about the corruption and payoffs of the Indian traders, implicating both Orvil Grant and Belknap. Custer's testimony was crucial to impeachment proceedings against Belknap, which infuriated President Grant, who canceled Custer's plan to return to Fort Lincoln to command his troops.

Without authorization, Custer left Washington in early May. Once he reached the headquarters of the Department of Dakota in St. Paul, he sent back a telegram to the President. "I have seen your order transmitted through the General of the Army directing that I be not permitted to accompany the expedition to move against the hostile Indians. As my entire regiment forms a part of the expedition and I am the senior officer of the regiment on duty in this department I respectfully, but most earnestly, request that while not allowed to go in command of the expedition I may be permitted to serve with my regiment in the field. I appeal to you as a soldier to spare me the humiliation of seeing my regiment march to meet the enemy and I not share its dangers." Because Grant was harshly criticized by the Democrats and the press for his treatment of Custer, he relented and allowed Custer to go with the Seventh Cavalry, although by then Terry had been appointed in his place as overall commander of the Dakota column.

XI

AS A RESULT OF THIS SITUATION, CUSTER never felt subordinate to General Terry, particularly now that Custer had found the Indians on his own and was in a position to attack. In fact, Custer had earlier told Colonel Ludlow of the Army Corps of Engineers that he was determined "to cut loose from, and make my operations independent of, General Terry during the summer" and that he had "got away from Stanley and would be able to swing clear of Terry" without any difficulty. It is therefore not surprising that when Bloody Knife told him early in the morning of June 25, 1876, that there were enough Sioux below to keep his men fighting for two or three days, Custer responded, "I guess we'll get through them in one day."

That morning, shortly after this brief conversation with Bloody Knife, Custer ordered his men to begin their march. They had already been on the move for over twenty-four hours, although perhaps Custer still expected to allow them to rest that afternoon and evening before attacking the following morning. The Seventh Cavalry marched for about ten miles and, around ten-thirty that morning, came to a deep, wooded ravine where Custer told his men to take cover and wait.

Custer then rode to the Crow's Nest to join Varnum and see for himself what the Indian scouts had been reporting to him. Varnum told Custer that his troops had been discovered and that he had seen hostiles fleeing back toward the village, presumably to inform the main body of Indians that a white army was approaching. Custer climbed to the top of the summit to see for himself. He looked down toward the valley but could see no signs whatsoever of the Indians. One of his scouts on the bluff with him, a half-breed named Mitch Bouyer who also interpreted for the Crow scouts, pointed down toward the valley and said the village was about fifteen miles distant and the largest encampment of hostile Indians he had ever seen. Custer used his field glasses and looked. "I still can't see them!" he said. Bouyer and the others insisted that the Indians were there.

While Custer was gone, other scouts returned and reported to officers at the ravine that the troops had been discovered by the Sioux. A Sergeant Curtis received permission to retrieve some boxes of hard bread left on the trail. Curtis returned and reported to Captain Yates that he saw a hostile Indian bending over the bread box trying to open it. Yates relayed this information to Captain Keogh who, in turn, related it to Custer's brother, Tom Custer, who then rode to meet Custer coming back from the Crow's Nest. Before reaching his men, then, Custer knew that, not only had his troops been discovered from the front of the column, but that hostiles had also encircled his rear.

Still, Custer had not seen the village himself. It was already hot and perhaps the gathering haze had obscured his view. Nevertheless, Custer made the decision to attack the Indian village at once. Unlike the Battle of the Washita, where he had successfully led a column of armed men against a village of Indians, this time Custer was not attacking at dawn in the dead of winter, but, rather, at midday in the height of summer. Not surprisingly, there has been much discussion whether the village need have been attacked at all. In 1919, a Miniconjou tribesman and veteran of the battle said to General H. L. Scott, "If Custer had come up and talked with us, we had all agreed we would have surrendered and gone in with him." Similar statements by other Indians confirm this. Later, General Scott admitted that negotiating with the Indians, rather than fighting them, had not been considered a viable option at the time of the Battle of the Little Bighorn.

A Sioux chief named Pretty Voice Eagle spoke with Custer before the army had left Fort Lincoln and asked Custer to promise that he would not fight his people. "We asked him to raise his hand to God that he would not fight the Sioux, and he raised his hand. After he raised his hand to God that he would not fight the Sioux he asked me to go west to my delegation to see these roaming Sioux, and tell them to come back to the reservation, that he would give them food, horses and clothing.... If Custer had given us time we would have gone out ahead of him, but he did not give us time."

Years before, Custer smoked a peace pipe with Medicine Arrow, a Cheyenne chief whose village lay on a branch of the Red River in Texas. Through sign language, Medicine Arrow told Custer that he wanted peace. Custer agreed. Medicine Arrow said that should he, Custer, ever make war again on the Cheyenne and break his promise of peace that he and all his men would be killed. To underscore his point, Medicine Arrow took the ashes of the peace pipe and tapped them out on Custer's boots. Another Cheyenne chief named Brave Bear was present at this meeting and likely took a keen interest in this white chief with the long curly hair. Brave Bear was at the Battle of the Washita and escaped Custer's bullets. Now, Brave Bear was camped with his people, the Cheyennes, along with the Sioux on the Little Bighorn River as Custer prepared his men to fight.

When Custer returned to his troops in the ravine, he promptly held another officers' meeting, informing his men that scouts had found the Indian village in the valley of the Little Bighorn. He also said their troops had been discovered both from the front and from the rear. This meant that any stealth Custer might have used would be wasted, though all the dust kicked up by his men and horses would have most likely given them away. Therefore, he intended to attack the village at once. Custer explained to his officers that he could not stick to his original plan of attacking at dawn on June 26, for his biggest fear was losing the Indians. None of the officers present objected to this change of plan. Custer then told the company commanders to assign one non-commissioned officer and six privates to accompany the mule pack train that carried their supplies. Further, he told these company commanders to prepare their men for battle, making sure each was properly supplied with ammunition. He would assign each company its place in the march in the order in which company commanders reported back to him. Custer also conferred with the Indian scouts and told them to ride on ahead and steal or stampede the Sioux pony herd.

An elder scout and leader of the Rees named Stabbed rode among his tribesmen, exhorting them to be brave. He then took some clay he had brought from Fort Lincoln and rubbed a little on the chest of each of his men to make "their hearts strong" in the coming battle. The Indians accompanying Custer held no illusions about what was to come. Bloody Knife had signed to the sun with his hands, "I shall not see you go down behind the hills tonight." Custer was told by one of his scouts that the biggest collection of Indians he had ever seen lay ahead. Custer himself did not pretend to think that he would fight a small or even moderate amount of hostiles. "The largest Indian camp on the North American continent is ahead," he told his officers, "and I am going to attack it."

There is a peculiar and haunting quality to the behavior of these military men as they prepared for battle in the heat of that Sunday afternoon—a robotic deliberateness—as if they were under the spell of the same group-think mentality that claimed the officers of the *Titanic* as the luxury liner plowed full steam ahead toward an ice field. Nowhere is the quality of this American military failure more poignant than in the disparity between the behavior of the whites and the behavior of the Indians as both prepared for the Battle of the Little Bighorn. Half Yellow Face, a Crow scout, told Custer, "You and I are both going home today by a road we do not know."

Inspections were made. The troops were ready. The column began to march. Shortly before noon, Custer's men crossed the divide that separated the valleys of the Rosebud and the Little Bighorn. A third of a mile beyond, at seven minutes after twelve noon, Custer halted his troops and made out battalion assignments. His total force consisted of thirty-one officers, 566 troopers, and fifty scouts and civilians. Major Reno would take troop "M" under Captain French, troop "A" under Captain Moylan and Lieutenant De Rudio, troop "G" under Lieutenants McIntosh and Wallace, as well as the Indian scouts under Lieutenants Varnum and Hare. Reno's total came to eleven officers, 129 men, and thirty-five others. Captain Benteen would take troop "H" under Lieutenant Gibson, troop "D" under Captain Weir and Lieutenant Edgerly, and troop "K" under Lieutenant Godfrey.

Benteen's total came to five officers and 110 men. Lieutenant Mathey commanded the pack train. He was escorted by troop "B" under Captain McDougall. The total for the pack train came to two officers and 127 men. Custer himself took troop "I" under Captain Keogh and Lieutenant Porter, troop "F" under Captain Yates and Lieutenant Reily, troop "C" under Captain Tom Custer and Lieutenant Harrington, troop "E" under Lieutenants Smith and Sturgis, and troop "L" under Lieutenants Calhoun and Crittenden. Custer's total—the largest of the four units—came to thirteen officers, two hundred men, and eight scouts.

From the reports of his scouts, Custer estimated that the Indian village was about fifteen miles away. His greatest concern was that the Indians would scatter and escape upon his approach. As in the Battle of the Washita, his intent was to keep his four units divided, surround the village with the three fighting units, and attack. Worried that the Indians might escape upstream, Custer ordered Benteen to take his troops to a line of bluffs about a mile to the west to look for any signs of Indians in the upper valley.

As Custer and Reno began their march in a direct line toward the village, Custer sent two additional orders via couriers to Benteen, whose column was still in sight. They first instructed Benteen to go to the second line of bluffs if the first set of bluffs had an obstructed view of the Indian village. The second order, dispatched after Custer had covered another mile, instructed Benteen to descend into the valley if he found no Indians once he reached the second line of bluffs. Custer and Reno, separated by a small creek, trotted only part of the time, worried that they might out-distance Benteen who was now in rougher terrain. About five miles from the divide, they quickened their pace. About two that afternoon, Custer sighted the remains of a lone teepee up ahead and waved Reno over to join him on the right bank of the creek. Custer halted before this teepee that had been set on fire by the scouts who were mortal enemies of the tribe to whom it had belonged. It contained the unburnt body of a dead warrior. Signs of a deserted village lay about it.

Custer likely examined the burned teepee, although hurriedly. Though he did not know him, the lone warrior inside was a Lakota named Old She

Bear. He had been killed in the battle with General Crook in which the Lakotas and Cheyennes had repulsed Crook's forces. Did Custer stare at the slain warrior, puzzled and anxious? Although the man was a warrior like himself, these burial symbols, including the Indian hieroglyphics, were foreign to him. Custer, in fact, was quite typical of the leaders of the United States Army, many of whom had very little understanding of Indian culture.

Perhaps some of the white civilians, bolstered by a New England sense of noblesse oblige, bore sincere concern and empathy for the Indians, and yet progress—white progress in the form of the railroad, and gold prospecting, and settlements, and clearing the land—took precedence. These military men had just fought and won a bloody Civil War to maintain the Union and they intended to finish the job—that is, its western expansion—with blood. There was no need to understand the Indian culture. In Canada, by contrast, there had been far less bloodshed—in fact, the mixing of white and Indian, epitomized by the peaceful success of the Hudson's Bay Company, occurred across a territory as large as the US without the fierce, vindictive battles executed along the Plains.

American military leaders had won this conflict with the Indians by employing a new doctrine of total war, aptly exercised by General Sherman in the Carolinas and Georgia, in which the disruption of the welfare, economy, and morale of an enemy's society constituted vital military objectives. In this they foreshadowed some of the haunting maxims of Clausewitz and that dark, Germanic hold over World War One. In a way, Custer's last battle commenced the violence of the Twentieth Century, and to some extent, set its tone. Here was a race war—much like the violence of World War Two and the late-Twentieth Century wars in the Balkans—in which the United States government's solution involved rounding up and isolating men, women, and children on a racial basis, and, if need be, killing them. Perhaps the most disturbing parallel was Hitler's decision to base his concentration camps on the model of the American Indian reservations. In addition, the much-heralded Lewis & Clark Expedition, viewed in its worst light, accomplished the means for our version of American *Lebensraum,* or "living space."

Custer looked blankly at the dead Indian in the teepee. Here was a white American warrior staring at another human being who had died in battle and yet there was no understanding, no connection. Nothing would bring these two together except death. "The brass hats are to blame for this,"

Senator Thomas Hart Benton told his colleagues in Washington, "sending school house officers and pot-house soldiers to treat the Indians as beasts and dogs."

One of Custer's men, the interpreter Gerard, interrupted the general's reverie by calling from a nearby knoll, "Here go your Indians, running like devils." He had seen a group of about forty or fifty warriors three miles away, cantering away from the column. This further reinforced in Custer's mind that the Indians were in flight. He ordered his Indian scouts to pursue the fleeing hostiles. They refused. Now, in the heat of midday, the scene began to take on a surreal quality. Custer was determined to fight yet he had no idea of the immense size of the hostile Indian village. Custer's officers and the men under them would follow his orders. The Indian scouts—knowing what lay ahead—made preparations for death.

Now Reno got specific orders, passed to him via Custer's adjutant, Lieutenant Cooke: "The village was only two miles above and running away; to move forward at as rapid a gait as prudent and to charge afterwards, and that the whole outfit would support you." At the time this order was given, Benteen was likely two to five miles behind and to the west of Custer and Reno. Therefore, in order to support the whole outfit, Custer's column would be forced to engage the enemy as well. But, as Reno descended down the hill and crossed the Little Bighorn at about 2:50 PM, Custer had turned north and was no longer near him. After Reno forded the river, he saw ahead of him the southern most lodges of a huge village. He sent Privates McIlhargy and Mitchell of Company L to Custer to warn him that the Indian village was not in flight after all, but actually massing for an attack.

By now, Custer had halted his column at a small stream to water his horses. His right-hand turn, due north, had taken him along the ridge above the valley. No doubt his intention was to attack the village on the opposite side from Reno. Custer received the reports from Reno's messengers, including Cooke, who had left Reno to rejoin Custer, that the Sioux were swarming upstream to meet Reno.

Custer ignored this news and kept his troops heading north for another one or two miles. A little after three that afternoon, from the crest of a bluff that overlooked the valley, he finally saw the size of the Indian village. There were thousands and thousands of Indian lodges and, to his left, Reno's small battalion charging toward this village along the valley floor. As the messengers had warned Custer, the Indians were not fleeing, as he had expected, but gathering to fight.

One certainly could not blame the Plains Indians for fighting both on this particular afternoon or at other times. Phil Sheridan once commented, in a rare moment of reflection, that the Plains Indians had been content until the arrival of Nineteenth Century progress, "or whatever it may be called . . . We took away their country and their means of support, broke up their mode of living, their habit of life, introduced disease and decay among them, and it was for this and against this that they made war. Could anyone expect less?"

Even though Custer trotted on for another mile to a still higher bluff, later called Weir Point, the view was still the same: thousands of Indians gathered to fight. Reno's battalion, rebuffed on its initial charge, was now forming a skirmish line. Absorbing severe casualties, Reno would soon retreat back across the river where Benteen would later join him. Even though many of their men were lost, Reno and Benteen would survive the battle. But Custer's day was different.

Now, under his direct command he had over two hundred men, and battle was imminent. He released his Indian scouts. They had done their job—they had found the Indians and now it was up to him to fight. During those strange moments, in the heat of mid-afternoon, Custer kept looking for Benteen and ordered the trumpeter, Giovanni Martini (an Italian who had recently anglicized his name to John Martin), to return to Benteen with a message. Because Martin spoke little English, Adjutant Cooke scribbled out the message on a page from his memorandum book—"Benteen. Come on. Big Village. Be quick. Bring packs. W. W. Cooke PS Bring packs." But, by then, it hardly mattered.

We leave Custer here—at this moment of his epiphany, when he finally understood the size of the Indian village, and realized he would likely fight his last battle. What happened to Custer that afternoon has entered the popular American imagination. We leave him along those bluffs, then, at Medicine Tail Coulee, where shortly before four that afternoon, the first shots of the Sioux and Cheyenne rang out in his direction.

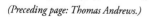
(Preceding page: Thomas Andrews.)

THE SHORT,
HAPPY LIFE OF
THOMAS ANDREWS

I

THE TITANIC BRUSHED AN ICEBERG at 11:40 PM. Passengers noted a faint grinding noise emanating from below and lasting less than thirty seconds. Captain Edward Smith, a white-bearded veteran of the White Star Line, rushed to the bridge and began cracking off orders. Reports from his engineers below indicated serious trouble. Smith summoned Thomas Andrews, managing director of the Harland & Wolff shipyard, the *Titanic's* builder. Andrews understood the *Titanic* better than anyone, and the Captain requested he sound the ship.

Andrews descended the crew's stairway to attract less attention and inspected first the mailroom and the nearby squash court (water lapped against the foul line on the backboard), and then boiler rooms five and six. He then ascended through the A Deck foyer, where a group of passengers studied his face to detect the gravity of the problem.

Just outside the bridge, the ship's builder and her captain conferred beneath a star-filled sky. Smith stared hard at Andrews. In a quiet voice, Andrews explained. The wounds from the iceberg covered over two hundred feet. The first five watertight compartments were flooding. A sixth was damaged. The bulkheads between each compartment did not create a complete seal. In fact, the bulkhead between the fifth and sixth compartments went only as high as E Deck. The *Titanic* could float if any two or three of these compartments were flooded. It could even float with four compartments flooded. If the first five compartments flooded, however, the pull of the water would force the bow of the ship to start sinking. Once that happened, water in the fifth compartment would flow over the bulkhead into the sixth and then, as the bow continued down, water in the sixth compartment would flow into the seventh and so on. Andrews knew the *Titanic's* doom was a mathematical certainty. As if to underscore his explanation, the ship began to list slightly, almost imperceptibly, toward the bow.

Captain Smith raised his eyes heavenward. He was fifty-nine years old and had planned to retire after this trip. In fact, he would have retired sooner, but he traditionally took the White Star ships on their maiden voyages. It was his greatest boast to be alive and active in a time when shipbuilding had reached its zenith. Earlier he had said, "I cannot conceive any condition which would cause a ship to founder. I cannot conceive of any vital disaster happening to this vessel. Modern shipbuilding has gone beyond that."

Now it was clear to both men that the ship would sink, and they would not live to see the morning. We imagine the two of them lingering for a few moments, as if, by parting, they would trigger the events that would cause more than fifteen hundred men, women, and children to drown in a cold and dark sea.

II

ON SUNDAY, APRIL 14, 1912, AT APPROXIMATELY 9:00 AM, the Cunard ocean liner, *Caronia*, sent a wireless to Captain Smith. It said: "Captain, Titanic—West Bound steamers report bergs, growlers, and field ice in 42 N from 49 to 50 W."

This was not the first ice warning sent to the *Titanic's* wireless room during its voyage from Southampton to New York, but certainly the *Caronia's* was the most significant. Fourth Officer Joseph Boxhall wrote the single word "ice" on a slip of paper above the coordinates noted by the *Caronia* and then tucked the paper into a frame above the chart room table. Third Officer Herbert Pittman remembered seeing the *Caronia's* message. Around noon, Captain Smith showed the warning to Second Officer Charles Lightoller. Other ice warnings had filtered into the *Titanic's* chain of command. The French ship *La Touraine* had warned of ice on April 12; the *Rappahannock* had actually signaled the *Titanic* that ice lay ahead on the night of April 13. But the *Caronia's* message was noted down, placed appropriately on the ship's chart room table, observed, discussed. No need to worry, however. Captain Smith was one of the North Atlantic's best, taking his final voyage before retirement, on one of the largest and safest sea-going vessels then built.

Modern shipbuilding, at least as far as the White Star Line was concerned, began at the shipyards of Harland & Wolff in Belfast, Northern Ireland. The backbone of the company, William James Pirrie, had joined Harland & Wolff as an apprentice draftsman in 1863 at the age of fifteen, became a full partner in 1874, and had assumed the post of managing director in 1895. In 1907, at a dinner party in London with the head of the White Star Line, J. Bruce Ismay, Pirrie and Ismay hatched a plan to build three ocean liners, each of which was to be larger and more luxurious than any of the ships owned by the White Star's chief rival, the powerful Cunard Line.

Harland & Wolff's business relationship with White Star had been happy and fruitful from the beginning. Gustav Wolff was the nephew of Gustavus Schwabe, the man whose capital had helped Bruce Ismay's father, Thomas Ismay, start the company in the first place. Moreover, White Star allowed Harland & Wolff to build her ships on a cost-plus basis: White Star could be assured that all details would be attended to; Harland & Wolff would make a profit. Competition between Cunard and White Star was fierce. Cunard ships, made in Glasgow, were faster; White Star ships, more luxurious. The North Atlantic trade, with its flow of immigrants to the New World, could support both even when the upstart Germans got into the business in the 1890s. The plan hatched at the London dinner party to build three new liners was expedited by White Star's enviable financial situation.

In 1902, Ismay had sold the White Star Line to J. Pierpont Morgan who added this shipping concern to others he had purchased under the umbrella company called International Mercantile Marine, or IMM. Harland & Wolff's Pirrie, who happened to be a member of the British board of IMM, and who had helped Morgan with earlier acquisitions, prompted the sale of White Star to the American millionaire. Pirrie persuaded young Ismay to sell his family's business because he wanted the advantages that Morgan's fabulous wealth would offer. In addition, Ismay kept his post as managing director of White Star and, because of his organizational abilities, eventually became president of IMM. Therefore, all was well on that summer evening in 1907 when Pirrie and Ismay dreamed of their three beautiful ships. Each would be nearly fifty percent larger than the *Lusitania*, the star of the Cunard line; each would be a hundred feet longer. One was to be called *Olympic*. One was to be called *Titanic*. The third would be called *Britannic*. Of the three, the *Titanic* was to be the largest and the most luxurious.

Perhaps the ship's enormous size brought a sense of tranquility to the officers of the *Titanic* on Sunday, April 14. With a passenger capacity of nearly three thousand, the *Titanic* was equipped with the highest luxuries of Edwardian sea travel: spacious dining areas, a gymnasium, a pool, first class luxury suites, an oak-paneled grand staircase illuminated by a glass dome, smoking rooms with leather furniture and Oriental rugs, an outdoor French cafe with an adjoining "boulevard." In addition, the *Titanic's* passengers were treated to plentiful deck space for recreation, a condition Ismay had sought during the ship's construction in lieu of, among other things, extra lifeboats. Captain Rostron of the *Carpathia* later said that a ship of this kind was "practically unsinkable . . . a lifeboat in itself."

Certainly, Captain Smith believed that the ship was unsinkable. Ice warnings were noted but perhaps not taken seriously. Moreover, the Marconi system with its wireless messages was relatively new in 1912. A ship's captain must see the dangerous conditions himself and then take appropriate action. In addition, up until commanding the *Titanic*, Captain Smith's record sailing the Atlantic had been flawless. He had begun his career aboard a clipper ship in 1869, had joined the White Star Line in 1880 as fourth officer on the *Celtic* (note how White Star ships end with an "ic" and Cunard liners an "ia"), and had achieved command of the *Republic* in 1887. He had commanded numerous White Star vessels, and nearly all of them had sailed without a hitch.

III

NOW, EARLY IN THE AFTERNOON OF APRIL 14, while many of the passengers finished an elegant luncheon, Captain Smith studied another "ice" message, this one from fellow White Star liner, *Baltic*. "Captain Smith, Titanic. Have had moderate variable winds and clear fine weather since leaving. Greek steamer *Athinai* reports passing iceberg and large quantities of field ice today in 41°51' north latitude, 49°52' west longitude."

Two or three minutes later, as Captain Smith carried this message to A Deck, the German liner, *Amerika*, chimed in with the news that she had passed two large icebergs at 41°27' north latitude, 50°8' west longitude. Captain Smith descended from the bridge to the Promenade Deck where he discovered Bruce Ismay, the head of the White Star Line, cheerful and ebullient, talking to passengers George and Eleanor Widener along the starboard railing. Smith passed the *Baltic's* message to Ismay. Ismay studied the message, then pocketed it before going to lunch.

Later that afternoon, Ismay encountered Mrs. John B. Thayer and Mrs. Arthur Ryerson—two socially prominent Pennsylvania women—and showed them the *Baltic's* ice message. In passing he also discussed how he expected the *Titanic* to make excellent time on her trip to New York. "We are not going very fast," he said. "Twenty or twenty-one knots, but we are going to start up some new boilers this evening." Just before dinner Ismay returned the *Baltic's* message to Captain Smith, who wanted it posted for his officers to read. By this time the temperature of the water was for-ty-three degrees.

Earlier, perhaps around 5:30 or 5:45 PM, the Captain had ordered the ship to steam an additional sixteen miles southwest of its normal route, thus turning a deeper corner than normal. Such was a rudimentary pre-caution. In the bridge, Second Officer Lightoller started his 6:00 to 10:00 PM watch by asking Sixth Officer Moody to calculate when he expected the *Titanic* to encounter the ice. "I expect around eleven o'clock sir," Moody answered.

At 7:00 PM, Lightoller took dinner and was temporarily relieved by First Officer William Murdoch, who instructed Lamp Trimmer Samuel Hem-mings to darken certain forward lights on the ship since they might inhibit sightings of any icebergs. At 7:30 PM, Lightoller returned to the bridge. Noticing how cold it had grown since sundown, Lightoller ordered Quar-termaster Robert Hitchens to caution the *Titanic's* carpenter to keep an eye on the ship's fresh water lest it freeze. The temperature of the water was now thirty-nine degrees.

Down below on B Deck, in the à la carte restaurant, Captain Smith dined with a group of prominent Americans, including George and Elea-nor Widener, their son, Harry, Mr. and Mrs. John B. Thayer, their son, Jack, Mr. and Mrs. William E. Carter, and President Taft's aide-de-camp, Major Archibald Butt. In addition to managing the ship, Captain Smith acted as host to the passengers on board, particularly the wealthy ones. Such a role suited the Captain well. Always friendly and courteous, he had a way about him—a strong paternal presence, a reassuring manner. Tonight, Captain Smith was concerned about the ice, but not to the extent of actually ordering the vessel slowed. After all, he was a veteran on the Atlantic run, and had been sailing for decades, well before captains had the luxury of Marconi messages warning of ice. A good captain would see any obstacles first and then take precautions.

Certainly, Smith was right about the newness of the Marconi system. In 1894, in Beillese, Italy, a precocious twenty-year-old inventor named Guglielmo Marconi had begun to fiddle with an apparatus that would send Morse code messages without the aid of telegraph wires. Son of an Italian father and a Scotch-Irish mother, Marconi used the following years to both perfect his invention and secure its safe market. After circumventing competitors and well-intentioned regulations, Marconi consolidated his hold on ship-to-ship and ship-to-shore communications.

At the 1906 Berlin International Conference on Wireless Communication at Sea, participating countries decided that all ship stations and operators had to be licensed by their home countries. In addition, each ship was to have a three-letter call signature. The *Titanic* was designated MGY. Participants also negotiated an international distress call. The old call, which the British still preferred, was CQD. CQ meant "seek you" and the accompanying D was for "danger." However, some countries suggested SOS, not because it meant "Save Our Souls" or "Save Our Ship," but because SOS was so easy to hear through overlapping transmissions and interference.

Prior to the *Titanic,* the most publicized case of the usefulness of a Marconi system at sea happened in 1909 near Nantucket, the island off the coast of Massachusetts. There, on a foggy pre-dawn morning, the *Florida,* a passenger liner of the Lloyd Italiano Line, rammed a White Star ship called the *Republic.* The *Republic* was seriously damaged; the *Florida* less so. Pulling up beside the White Star ship, the *Florida* began to take on her passengers while the *Republic's* wireless operator, Jack Binns, worked feverishly to repair the wireless system that had been damaged in the collision. Because both vessels were helpless, and because the *Florida* traveled without wireless, salvation depended upon Binns restarting his wireless, a feat he accomplished several hours later. Ships came to the rescue. Binns achieved instant fame, and the Marconi system gained public confidence.

In the early part of the Twentieth Century, sea travel across the Atlantic was big business, and Marconi made it easy for the shipping companies to adopt his system. The White Star Line, for example, did not actually have to purchase a wireless set. Instead, Marconi leased his equipment and rented out his operators. Technically, then, the *Titanic's* two wireless operators, Jack Phillips and Harold Bride, were Marconi men and not employees of the White Star Line. When the *Titanic* departed Southampton on 10 April 1912, she carried Marconi equipment with a daytime range of two-hundred-and-fifty to four hundred miles and a nighttime range of over two thousand miles.

The ship's electrical systems powered the Marconi apparatus. A battery-operated backup system was also on board. Phillips, twenty-five, and Bride, twenty-two, spent most of their shipboard hours confined to the wireless cabin located near the bridge. Phillips and Bride worked separate shifts so that the system could be manned day and night, but it is worth noting that many ships carried only one wireless operator who usually shut his system down at the end of his shift. In 1912, no international regulation required vessels to maintain round-the-clock wireless. Phillips and Bride were paid respectively fifteen and twenty dollars a month, the low pay offset by the interesting nature of the job. They were required to work long hours. They did not socialize with the officers of the ship, nor did they wear a White Star uniform. They had their own uniform—the clothing of a Marconi Marine. The White Star Line expected them to send and receive messages twenty-four hours a day; the din of Morse messages kept them busy, whether it was the faint crackle of a distant ship or the deafening sound of one nearby.

The wireless men that worked the Atlantic route knew one another—each had a particular style in transmitting messages. Their communications with one another consisted largely of abbreviations: the official "Q" code being supplemented by unofficial substitutes. The motive was always to deliver the message with as few characters as possible. For example: QRA meant, "What is the name of your station?" And the response, QRA MGY, "The name of my station is the Titanic." TU OM GN, "Thank you, old man, good night!" GM OM—"Good morning, old man." GN OM—"Good night, old man." Frequently used: GTH OM QRT—"Go to hell, old man, keep quiet, I'm busy." Or simply: QRT—"Keep quiet, I'm busy."

The officer on watch was expected to take a navigational reading from the stars. Three stars for latitude and three stars for longitude while the Third Officer on this particular night was expected to operate the chronometer and note the exact time if called to do so. On this night, Fifth Officer Lowe was busy calculating the miles per hour of the ship as well as working out her exact position at 8:00 PM for the captain.

Lowe left the completed report on the chart room table, so that the ship's position might be filled into the night order book. At noon, Lowe glanced at the course laid off on the chart and surmised that, judging from the distance run, they had held their course for about three-quarters-of-an-hour after reaching "the corner"—the approximate area of ocean where a ship would shift course to accommodate the curvature of the earth. On a Mercator chart, the rhumb, or straight line of the course, is the shortest distance between two points. On a globe, however, the shortest distance between any two points is the arc of a Great Circle, which, if carried round the globe, would divide the earth into two equal portions and whose plane would always pass through the earth's center.

On a Mercator chart, the ship's track is represented by a rhumb line that cuts each meridian at the same angle. A Great Circle track between any two points on a Mercator chart is therefore represented by a curve and the vessel steered from one to the other along the rhumbs, or straight lines, joining them. In Great Circle sailing, frequent alterations of course are necessary so that the vessel's track may coincide as nearly as possible with the Great Circle. Great Circle sailing is principally of use between places in high latitudes, where it shortens trips. The track to be followed by the *Titanic* on her passage to New York was laid out by the commander on the large chart spread out on the table in the navigating room. As Lowe examined the chart, he reasoned the ship's course ought to have been altered earlier, at about five o'clock that afternoon. Of course, the quickest means by which to determine the course of the *Titanic* lay in the narrow walls of the wireless room.

Prior to the *Titanic's* fateful Sunday, the ship's Marconi system began to act up. Late in the night of Friday, April 12, transmission became difficult. Phillips and Bride traced the problem to leads running from the transformer to the transmitter. The leads had burned through their protective coating and had made contact with iron bolts supporting the equipment, thus depleting the system of power.

Phillips did the lion's share of the work to fix the short. Again another ice message agitated the wireless set, this one from the liner, *Mesaba*. Precisely what happened to this ice message has been the subject of speculation, but very likely, Phillips took the message, placed it under a nearby paperweight, and continued transmitting to Cape Race, Newfoundland, his first opportunity that night to transmit messages to and from the American continent. The *Mesaba's* sender assumed that the message would be immediately delivered to Captain Smith as it contained important navigational coordinates: "From

Mesaba to *Titanic*. Ice report in lat. 42°N to 41°25' N, long. 49° to 50°30' W saw much heavy pack ice and a great number large icebergs. Also field ice weather good, clear." In other words, these coordinates translated to ice dead ahead. Not only did Captain Smith not respond to this message, as the *Mesaba* operator expected him to, chances are he never even saw the message.

In Walter Lord's recap of the *Titanic* disaster, *The Night Lives On*, written nearly thirty years after his first book on the subject, *A Night to Remember*, the author revisits the subject of lackluster procedures between the ship's bridge and its wireless operations. Apparently, Fourth Officer Boxhall did not thoroughly read the one ice message he saw. In addition, Fifth Officer Lowe claimed that he saw the ice warnings collected under the chit above the chart room table but took notice only to the extent that he confirmed that the ship would reach ice on someone else's watch. Third Officer Pittman said he glanced "casually" at the ice warnings—that was it—and Second Officer Lightoller, scheduled to take command when the ship began cutting through colder waters, never saw the chit containing the ice warnings. Lightoller and Sixth Officer Moody even discussed the likelihood of the *Titanic* encountering ice that evening. It was Moody's opinion that the ship would reach icebergs around 11:00 PM. Lightoller calculated in his own mind that the time would be closer to 9:30 PM, but he never bothered to correct the junior officer.

Lightoller was an experienced seaman. He had begun his career on sailing ships. This particular trip on board the *Titanic* was routine, placid, a luxury. The sea was calm and flat, a black mirror reflecting a moonless night sky etched with stars. He had witnessed much more difficult times at sea and had once been shipwrecked on a deserted island. Like the other members of the crew, Lightoller possessed a serene confidence.

IV

EVERY MEMBER OF THE TITANIC'S CREW exhibited a casual disregard of the ice warnings. In this, it seemed as if the crew were all thinking alike, as if this common ground in their thinking spelled the ship's doom. This group outlook—or "groupthink" as Professor Irving L. Janis described it in his book *Victims of Groupthink: A psychological study of foreign policy decisions and fiascoes*—contributes significantly to disaster, particularly when well-trained and well-meaning men act in concert and without dissent. Janis provides the example of Pearl Harbor, an event in which we find many parallels to the *Titanic* disaster.

During the autumn of 1941, the commander of the American naval forces at Pearl Harbor was Admiral Husband E. Kimmel, a serious, straightforward workaholic. Kimmel surrounded himself with a competent staff, and—like Captain Smith and his crew on the *Titanic*—Kimmel and his staff tended to think alike. Just as the crew of the *Titanic* was bombarded with ice messages during its voyage, Kimmel and his staff received numerous messages from Washington that hostilities with the Japanese were imminent.

On November 24, 1941, the chief of naval operations in Washington, Admiral Harold Stark, sent Kimmel a warning that war with Japan could break out at any time. "Chances of favorable outcome of negotiations with Japan very doubtful. This situation coupled with statements of Japanese government and movements of their naval and military forces indicated attack on Philippines or Guam is a possibility."

Kimmel's staff went further than the crew of the *Titanic*—they actually discussed the implications of the war warning. But Kimmel's men continued to believe that Pearl Harbor would not be a target of the Japanese. Next came a warning on November 27, 1941: "This dispatch is to be considered a war warning. Negotiations with Japan looking toward stabilization of conditions in the Pacific have ceased and an aggressive move by Japan is expected within the next few days. . . . Execute appropriate defensive deployment preparatory to carrying out the tasks assigned in WPL 46." This last bit was the naval war plan.

Again Kimmel discussed this warning with his staff, and all agreed that Pearl Harbor was not a possible target. Rather, they felt the Japanese would strike probably at Guam or the Philippines. Like Captain Smith and his crew, who felt they would be able to see the iceberg with enough time to steer clear of it, Admiral Kimmel and his staff felt so strongly that Pearl Harbor would not be a target that they were comfortable with the limited reconnaissance precautions already in place. In other words, they avoided even a minimum of extra precautions—including a partial increase in surveillance with some dispersal of warships, cancellation of weekend leaves, and full alert of anti-aircraft units—all of which would have gone far to saving lives.

On December 3, 1941, the United States learned that the Japanese had ordered all her embassies in America and other countries to destroy their secret codes. Kimmel and his men decided this move stemmed from the Japanese desire to take a routine precaution in case their embassies and consulates in British or American territory were seized in retaliation for their invasion of Thailand or Malaya. In each discussion about these warnings, Kimmel's group agreed that Pearl Harbor would not be a target. Like the crew of the *Titanic*, there was no dissension.

Moreover, both groups were very cohesive and shared strong feelings of loyalty to their leader. Kimmel's men played golf together. They played bridge with one another. They and their wives attended social events and dinner parties together. In fact, even their wives exhibited the same kind of complacent thinking—with one exception. On the night of December 6, 1941, Kimmel attended a dinner party given by Rear Admiral H. Fairfax Leary and his wife. Many members of Kimmel's staff and their wives were present. Seated next to Admiral Kimmel was Fanny Halsey, wife of Admiral Halsey, who had left Hawaii a few days earlier. During the dinner discussion, Mrs. Halsey stated that she was certain the Japanese were going to attack Pearl Harbor any time. "She was a brilliant woman," said Captain Joel Brunkley who later described the dinner party, "but everybody thought she was crazy."

Earlier that afternoon, Kimmel had been impressed by a particularly strong war warning, and had expressed concerns to his staff about the safety of his fleet. A staff member had promptly reassured the Admiral that "the Japanese could not possibly be able to proceed in force against Pearl Harbor when they had so much strength concentrated in their Asiatic operations." Another staffer told him no additional precautions were necessary. "We finally decided that what we had already done was still good and we would stick to it."

Just as Captain Smith exhibited a fatal complacency during the hours leading up to his disaster—note that he never told his crew to reduce the speed of the ship into the ice field—so, too, Admiral Kimmel failed to take even the minimum precautions against a possible Japanese attack of Pearl Harbor. How does one explain this?

Like Captain Smith, Admiral Kimmel operated under a set of assumptions he thought at the time perfectly valid, assumptions that prevented him from taking the needed precautions. Remember, both in the case of the *Titanic* and Pearl Harbor, we are looking back through the veil of the disaster. But Captain Smith and Admiral Kimmel didn't have that luxury when they were making decisions. Hindsight betrays Smith and Kimmel in harsher light than they deserve. Both *had* enjoyed successful careers. Based on a lifetime's experience of safe, uneventful Atlantic crossings, Captain Smith believed he could slow his ship down once he got to the ice and that he would have time to see the ice before hitting it. It was common practice among liner captains at the time to run their ships through the Atlantic nearly as fast as they could go.

Sadly, Kimmel and his staff also operated under the fatal combination of bad premises and terrific cohesiveness. Each man brought to the table an *esprit de corps* based on camaraderie and wishful thinking. Like the crew of the *Titanic*, they wanted to bring about the best possible outcome for their leader, and all tended to think alike. On December 1, 1941, Kimmel expressed concern to Lieutenant Commander Layton about the puzzling loss of radio contact with the Japanese aircraft carriers and asked Far East Command to retrieve additional information about them.

The next day, when the Admiral was again discussing the lost carriers with Layton, Kimmel remarked jokingly, "What, you don't know where the carriers are? Do you mean to say that they could be rounding Diamond Head and you wouldn't know it?" Layton responded more seriously that he hoped the carriers would be sighted well before that. But the joke had its point—at that very moment the Japanese carriers were indeed headed toward Diamond Head—and the conversation illuminated the fatal atmosphere of genial complacency between Kimmel and his men.

Unlike Captain Smith, who did not live to suffer past his unexpected disaster, Admiral Kimmel survived the bombing of Pearl Harbor and was subjected to a lengthy and excruciating investigation afterwards. When the planes swooped down from the sky on that Sunday morning, Kimmel knew immediately what had happened, and he told his staff that he would likely be relieved of his command.

Preceded by desultory submarine attacks, the Japanese onslaught on Pearl Harbor began about 8:00 AM on Sunday, December 7, when many of the military men were either in their bunks or on leave. Japanese aircraft were able to drop their bombs on ninety-six undefended ships in the harbor. They sank or damaged all eight battleships as well as three cruisers and four other vessels. More than two thousand men were killed, the bulk of them Navy personnel. More than two thousand men were missing or wounded. In addition, most of the Navy buildings and army aircraft installations were destroyed. During the heat of battle, Kimmel stood with one of his subordinate officers at his headquarters on the base when a bullet crashed through the glass of a window and grazed Kimmel, leaving a darkened path on his white uniform. He stooped down, picked up the spent bullet, and said, "It would have been merciful had it killed me." Kimmel was relieved of his command.

V

ON THE NIGHT OF APRIL 14, 1912, a night of perfect calm, Second Officer Lightoller gazed through the windows at the bridge and discovered a sea that would not challenge him. Yes, there was the probability that the ship would encounter ice, but there would be time—time to see and identify any iceberg, time to steer clear of it. It never occurred to Lightoller to advise Captain Smith to slow the ship's speed. After all, Lightoller had served under Smith on numerous transatlantic crossings. He had absolute confidence in his commander. "He was a great favorite, and a man any officer would give his ears to sail under. I had been with him many years, off and on, in the mail boats, and it was an education to see him con his own ship up through the intricate channels entering New York at full speed."

For his part, Captain Smith displayed serene self-assurance that evening. His ship cut through the calm, black water, a lighted palace set in motion. Everything seemed in order as he excused himself from the Wideners' party in the à la carte restaurant and made his way to the bridge. The time was about 9:00 PM. In addition to Lightoller (the senior officer on watch), Fourth Officer Boxhall and Sixth Officer Moody were on duty. When Captain Smith entered the bridge, he mentioned the cold. The side doors of the bridge were open to the weather.

"Yes, it is very cold, sir. In fact it is only one degree above freezing," replied Lightoller.

Both men peered into the night. Lightoller interjected an afterthought, "I have sent word down to the carpenter and rung up the engine room and told them that it will be freezing during the night."

"Very good," said Smith, continuing to look out into the blackness of the night. Then he said, "There is not much wind."

"No, it is a flat calm as a matter of fact."

"A flat calm?"

"Yes, quite flat. There is no wind."

Both men knew that no wind—a "flat calm" as they called it—meant that icebergs would be harder to see that night, even in the crystal clear air.

"When do you suppose we shall be reaching the ice?" asked Smith.

"An hour, perhaps more." Lightoller explained that the additional starlight might help illuminate any bergs. Even though there was no moon, the stars shone like a thousand diamonds spread irregularly upon a black blanket.

"Even if the berg shows a blue side, we will have enough time," said

Lightoller.

"Yes," said Smith. "We will have enough time."

The men gazed into the darkness for several more minutes. Captain Smith mentioned that if the weather should grow hazy they would have to slow the ship. As he prepared to retire, he told Lightoller, "If it becomes at all doubtful, let me know at once. I'll just be inside."

There is a peacefulness to this conversation, a muted tranquillity. Certainly, the *Titanic* set the tone of many of the Twentieth Century's significant transportation disasters, most notably the explosion and crash of the space shuttle *Challenger*, in which frozen O-rings allowed rocket fuel to escape and ignite.

On January 28, 1986, NASA launched the space shuttle *Challenger* during an unusual Florida cold spell. On board was Christa McAuliffe, a civilian schoolteacher, who brought to this mission the eager attention of school children across the nation. Prior to launch, Morton Thiokol, the contractor in charge of the solid rocket boosters (SRBs), had recommended against the launch because the company engineers felt the cold temperature might hamper the sealing capability of the O-rings that fitted between the casings of the two solid rocket boosters that propelled the space shuttle into orbit. But, after some discussion with the Marshall Space Flight Center, the NASA center responsible for the shuttle's entire propulsion system, Morton Thiokol changed its mind and recommended the launch.

What happened, of course, was a signal disaster before an unusually large television audience. A presidential commission was formed to investigate the disaster. Relatively soon, the commission began to focus on long-standing problems with the O-rings and the standard pre-launch review sessions in which Morton Thiokol had initially recommended against the launch. The commission focused on the solid rocket boosters—enormous propulsion systems (twelve feet in diameter and 159 feet high). The O-rings are like huge lengths of licorice joined at the ends so that they form a circle twelve feet across. They lie between the booster segments like the rubber ring between a Mason jar and its lid. Through a series of tests on earlier shuttles, Morton Thiokol engineers had concluded that cold weather had a detrimental effect on the sealing capabilities of the O-rings. In some cases, O-rings examined after shuttle launches (most SRBs could be retrieved) had shown significant erosion from hot gases. Thus the engineers' concerns about the cold weather were significant, and yet NASA managers, who had to make the ultimate call on whether to launch, decided to go ahead. This decision puzzled Diane Vaughan, author of *The Challenger*

Launch Decision. "It defied my understanding. If NASA managers launched Challenger because of production pressures, knowingly violating safety rules in the attempt to sustain the program's economic viability, how could they fail to take into account the extensive cost of an O-ring failure?"

In this particular case, O-ring erosion had happened before, though never to the extent of seriously endangering a mission. Therefore, even though the O-ring problem had been brought to the attention of the managers, they still decided to go ahead with the launch. The problem had not been corrected—there was, of course, risk—but the problem was not severe enough to stop the launch. In other words, the deviance had been accepted or normalized. In endeavoring to know why, two principal questions arise. One: Why, from 1977 to 1985, did NASA continue to accept the risk of a notable design flaw, tolerating more and more booster joint damage? And number two: Why did NASA launch the *Challenger* when the engineers who worked most closely with the O-rings were opposed?— Vaughan explores this concept of normalization of deviance.

"The attention paid to managers and rule violations after the disaster deflected attention from the compelling fact that, in the years preceding the Challenger launch, engineers and managers together developed a definition of the situation that allowed them to carry on as if nothing was wrong when they continually faced evidence that something was wrong. This is the problem of normalization of deviance. Further, risk is not a fixed attribute of some object, but constructed by individuals from past experience and present circumstances and conferred upon the object or situation. Individuals assess risk as they assess everything else—through the filtering lens of individual world view. A butcher at work, for example does not see the same immediate danger in the tools of that trade as does a parent catching a preschooler (who likely sees no danger at all) pulling a carving knife out of a kitchen drawer."

Likewise, in the *Titanic* disaster, Captain Smith and his crew bore little concern about allowing their ship to speed full-tilt into a known ice field because, in their experience, which was significant, they would have time to spot an iceberg and steer the vessel out of harm's way. In reviewing history, as Barbara Tuchman has observed, one needs to step back into the past. "According to Emerson's rule, every scripture is entitled to be read in the light of the circumstances that brought it forth. To understand the choices open to people of another time, one must limit oneself to what they knew, see the past in its own clothes, as it were, not in ours."

Both sets of circumstances—plowing at full speed into a known ice field and launching a space shuttle in subfreezing temperature when the craft had a known O-ring problem exacerbated by cold weather—seem preposterously dangerous, but only in hindsight.

At 6:00 AM on the morning of January 28, 1986, the *Challenger* crew were awakened. After breakfast they received a weather briefing. The temperature at that time was twenty-four degrees. The flight crew was told to expect a short delay because of two problems. First, there was ice on the launch pad. Second, the Launch Commit Criterion deemed that the outside temperature should be at least thirty-one degrees for the shuttle to be launched. Sometime after 8:00 AM, the seven-member crew got into their flight gear, boarded the spacecraft, and were strapped into their seats. Outside, the ice team inspected the launch pad for a second time. Even though the temperature had grudgingly climbed to thirty degrees, a cold wind continued to blow, freezing the water trickling out of the water system. One inspector, noting icicles along the stairwells in the fixed service tower, said that the scene "looked like something out of *Dr. Zhivago*."

The explosion of the shuttle *Challenger* shortly after lift-off was an unprecedented failure in the history of America's venture into space. True, there had been other incidents where lives were lost, but the *Challenger's* explosion in front of a huge television audience, many of whom were children, was the worst. This was failure—unequivocal, appalling, and spectacular. But, unlike the failure at the Battle of the Little Bighorn, in which the commander's judgment had been seriously flawed, the *Challenger* did not fail because a particular person (or even a group) had veered from standard procedure. In many ways, the *Challenger's* failure was closer to the *Titanic's*— an improper design, an untimely journey in cold weather. Still, the space shuttle failure bore a significant characteristic that sets it apart: the officials involved had followed the rules. Even during the hours and hours of grilling by members of the presidential commission looking into the disaster, Larry Mulloy, manager of the SRB program, kept reiterating, "We were absolutely relentless and Machiavellian about following through on all the required procedures at Level III." Why was there a breakdown? "With all procedural systems in place, we had a failure." This time, it was the rules that were in place that failed—as if we humans who construct these beautifully elaborate flying machines must expect failure arising from the machines' complexity alone.

VI

After Captain Smith left the bridge, Lightoller told Sixth Officer Moody to telephone the crow's nest and instruct the lookouts to keep an eye out for small ice and growlers and to pass the same on to the next lookouts, Fleet and Lee. Listening to the order conveyed, Lightoller asked Moody to re-send it since he had not mentioned the growlers. It was now 9:30 PM.

In the crow's nest, lookouts Archie Jewell and George Symons stared out at the darkness before them. "It is very cold here," said Jewell.

"Yes," said Symons, "by the smell of it there is ice about."

Jewell looked puzzled. "What do you mean by that?"

Symons replied, "As a rule you can smell ice before you get to it."

At a quarter to ten, according to schedule, Jewell and Symons greeted the new lookouts, Frederick Fleet and Reginald Lee, who had ascended the masthead ladder to the crow's nest. "Keep a sharp look-out for icebergs and growlers until daylight," said Symons to the new crew. Below, in the bridge, Quartermaster Robert Hitchens took over the wheel. Hitchens was accompanied by the new officer of the watch, First Officer William Murdoch, who came to relieve Lightoller.

"It is pretty cold," said Murdoch.

"Yes," said Lightoller, "it is freezing." It was then a little after 10:00 PM.

On the bridge of the *Titanic*, Lightoller and Murdoch stared ahead into the darkness. The First Officer and Second Officer of the ship discussed the smooth running of the ship's engines as well as the ice reports that had come through the wireless. "We might be up around the ice somewhere about eleven o'clock, I suppose," said Lightoller. Both men discussed the absence of definition between the horizon and the sea, a circumstance that would make spotting any iceberg that much more difficult, particularly if the blue side—that portion of the iceberg previously submerged—should be turned up.

Lightoller left Murdoch in command of the ship and descended first to the Boat Deck and then to A Deck, making his inspections. Most of the passengers by this time had turned in. In the wireless room, Phillips exchanged messages with the wireless operator at Cape Race, Walter Gray. Phillips praised the *Titanic* and relayed some of the more prominent names on her passenger list. At this time, the *Titanic's* speed had reached twenty-two-and-a-half knots.

At 11:00 PM, the wireless operator on board the Leyland liner, *Califor-*

nian, signaled to Phillips that ice lay in the path of the *Titanic*. The *Californian* had encountered enough ice to warrant her captain stopping the ship for the night. Unfortunately, the wireless transmission from the *Californian* was so close that it struck loudly into Phillips' ear and he replied, "Shut up. Shut up. I am busy; I am working Cape Race." Like some of the other warnings, the ice message from the *Californian* never reached the bridge. Phillips had been too busy—so busy, in fact, that his assistant, Harold Bride, intended to relieve Phillips at midnight rather than at 2:00 AM as was expected.

In the crow's nest of the *Titanic*, lookouts Fleet and Lee gazed into the darkness and noted that the surface of the sea was developing a slight haze. By then—a few minutes after 11:30 PM—the air was several degrees below freezing. Below, in the bridge, Sixth Officer Moody was inside the wheelhouse standing beside Quartermaster Hitchens at the wheel. Near them, Quartermaster Alfred Olliver adjusted the light on the compass. On the open part of the bridge, First Officer William Murdoch stood alone and stared before him at the sea. None of the men spoke.

There was a muted tranquility on board the ship bridge. Civil aviation accidents, in which sturdy, dependable jet aircraft crash due to a complex sequence of events, reveal eerie parallels to the *Titanic* accident, particularly in that serene calmness on the bridge or in the cockpit during those final moments preceding the disaster. Take, for example, the case of USAir Flight 427, a Boeing 737 that went down on its approach to Pittsburgh Airport in 1994.

Forty-five-year-old Peter Germano commanded Flight 427. He was assisted by First Officer Charles Emmett, a good-humored, thirty-eight-year-old Texan. Two USAir mechanics did a routine double-check of the plane after it landed at Chicago's O'Hare Airport. Flight 427 departed the gate at 6:02 PM and became airborne eight minutes later. Expected flying time to Pittsburgh was fifty-five minutes. Forty-five minutes into the flight, personnel at the Cleveland Air Route Traffic Control Center cleared Flight 427 to descend to ten thousand feet. As with the bridge of the *Titanic*, the mood inside the cockpit was untroubled and easy-going. Germano and Emmett chatted amiably and one of the stewardesses brought Emmett a fruit drink to which he jokingly asked to have rum added.

Approximately fifty minutes into the flight, Cleveland's air traffic center told Germano and Emmett to contact Pittsburgh's air traffic control for instructions as to their approach. After allowing a Delta 727 to approach before the USAir Flight, the Pittsburgh tower told Flight 427 to descend to six thousand feet and to keep an eye out for another aircraft, a private Jetstream, ascending near them. In response to the instruction about looking for the Jetstream, Captain Germano replied, "We're looking for traffic." Twenty seconds later, Emmett said in a mock German accent, "Oh, ya, I see zuh Jetstream." It was at this moment—when Emmett uttered the first syllable of the word "Jetstream"—that Flight 427 encountered its "upset," or what may better be termed "deviation."

In other words, the normal pattern and sequence of the plan had been altered, not by human decision or error, but by mechanical mishap. If the Twentieth Century is marked by its startling failures, certainly those failures transpire because of a series of mistakes. Deviation is the most prominent link in this chain. Eventually, deviation is followed by historical epiphany. When the principal actors in the drama realize that the deviation is severe enough to prevent reinstatement of their normal plan of operation under any circumstances, they have then discovered epiphany—the sudden illumination of permanently changed circumstances. As we have already seen, George Armstrong Custer discovered this deviation the moment he saw the size of the Sioux village he was about to attack. The overwhelming number of Sioux warriors meant he would no longer be able to execute his plan of military action. At this moment, deviation became epiphany.

VII

ALTHOUGH FLIGHT 427 DOES NOT GARNER THE SAME NOTORIETY as the disaster of the *Titanic*, the flight nevertheless reveals the drama inherent in a sudden, catastrophic change. Germano and Emmett knew they had lost complete control of the aircraft approximately eight seconds after the deviation. The cockpit sounded a cacophony of safety alarms, including the traffic alert and collision avoidance system sounding "traffic, traffic." By then, Flight 427 was in a nosedive and the aircraft was nearly vertical. Just before the 737 slammed straight into the ground at 301 miles per hour, Emmett could be heard saying simply, "No."

Thomas Andrews, our hero in the *Titanic* story, had more time to understand the nature of his epiphany. He boarded the ship with confidence. When the *Titanic* left Southampton and arrived at Cherbourg, he wrote his wife, "We reached here in a nice time and took on board quite a number of passengers. The two little tenders looked well, you will remember we built them about a year ago. We expect to arrive at Queenstown about 10:30 AM tomorrow. The weather is fine and everything is shaping up for a good voyage."

In his own mind, Andrews had planned for every contingency, every possible problem. A rather curious passage in *A Night To Remember* describes how Andrews had designed the writing room so that the women in first class could retire there after dinner, but he discovers that the modern women of the Twentieth Century "just wouldn't retire." Part of the writing room, therefore, could be converted into two more staterooms. It was this attention to detail that distinguished Andrews. His photograph reveals a face that is resolute, eyes marked with fierce determination. Here is a man who accomplished with thoroughness and industry each task to which he was assigned. His stateroom on board the ship was filled with charts. And there he would sit in concentration making notes for improvements. When he was not in his stateroom, he was walking about the ship with his workmen trying to discover and fix any imperfections. And yet he lacked the vision to foresee the most significant imperfection of all—that a continuous series of small punctures from an iceberg would fill at least five watertight compartments with seawater.

On Sunday night, Andrews had dinner and afterwards thanked the baker for some special bread he had baked. Andrews returned to his stateroom where he changed back into working clothes before sitting down at his desk to write.

Meanwhile, in the crow's nest of the *Titanic*, lookouts Fleet and Lee stared out to sea. They had no binoculars, an oversight that had somehow occurred when the ship left Queenstown. At an interval in time near 11:35 PM, Frederick Fleet saw an object looming in the darkness ahead. Without taking any time to determine just exactly what it was, Fleet reached across Lee for the crow's nest bell and rang it three times, a procedure that indicated an object dead ahead. He then grabbed the telephone to the bridge. "Is someone there?" asked Fleet.

"Yes," said Sixth Officer Moody. "What do you see?"

"Iceberg right ahead!"

Moody immediately conveyed the news to First Officer Murdoch. By then Murdoch had already seen the berg himself and rushed to the engine room telegraph. As he signaled "full speed astern" to the engine room, he ordered Hitchens, "Hard a' starboard"—that Hitchens should crank the wheel to the right, clockwise, which would actually cause the ship to turn left, toward port, as ships were designed to do back then.

"Hard a' starboard. The helm is hard over, sir," said Moody from his position behind Hitchens.

As the men on board the *Titanic* watched the iceberg looming closer and closer, the bow of the ship finally began to swing slowly left. At that point, Murdoch ordered, "Hard a' port," intending to bring the stern away from the ice. It was too late. With a sickening shudder, the starboard side of the bow scraped the berg. Pieces of ice fell onto the forecastle and well deck. Murdoch rang the alarm for the watertight doors below and then threw the automatic switch from the bridge that would shut them. A moment later Captain Smith rushed onto the bridge. "What have we struck?"

Murdoch stared back at the captain. "An iceberg, sir. I put her hard a' starboard and ran the engines full astern, but it was too close. She hit it. I intended to port around it, but she hit before I could do anymore."

The captain responded, "Close the watertight doors."

"The watertight doors are closed, sir," replied Murdoch.

"Did you sound the warning bell?"

"Yes."

VIII

IN THE CASE OF FLIGHT 427, NO OVERRIDING CAUSE was ever established although investigators suspected a malfunction of the plane's yaw stabilizer—a device on the plane's rudder that automatically helps to correct the effects of unintended horizontal movements of the plane's nose during flight. However, unlike Flight 427, where a mechanical malfunction caused the plane to crash, in the case of the *Titanic*, human error was as much to blame as the failure of technology. It was Captain Smith's decision, after all, to maintain approximately twenty-two knots as the ship headed into a known ice field. Moreover, men had built this ship; men had made the decisions on its design and safety features. In particular, one man—Thomas Andrews—had the overall responsibility for the construction of the *Titanic*.

Andrews came from a distinguished Ulster clan. His biographer, Shan Bullock, delivers an affectionate portrait of Andrews in his book, *A Titanic Hero: Thomas Andrews, Shipbuilder*, and notes that the Andrews family had been prominent for many generations in the village of Comber near Belfast. "The connection to Lord Pirrie, managing director of the White Star line, came when, in 1870, Thomas Andrews married Eliza Pirrie, a descendent of the Scotch Hamiltons, Lord Pirrie's sister, and herself a woman of the noblest type. To these, and of such excellent stock, was born, on February 7th, 1873, a son, named after his father, and described in the family record as Thomas Andrews of Dunallan."

Such was the lineage of the *Titanic's* builder. Thomas Andrews was an Irish lad who, early on, developed a fondness for boats and who garnered the admiration of his colleagues. Andrews fit his role well. He did not shirk from hard work, nor did he want the fruits of his labors tainted by favoritism. Like Custer, he was self-made.

Lord Pirrie decided early on that no special favor would be shown to his nephew. Andrews would have to succeed or fail on his own.

Failure, failure, failure—this was not on Andrews' mind as he embarked on his shipbuilding career. He spent his weekday nights in Belfast, near the shipyard. He rose ten minutes before five and was at work by six. He studied at night—machine and freehand drawing, applied mechanics, naval architecture. He was seldom in bed before eleven. He avoided reading novels and didn't bother with the newspapers. Rarely did he join his friends for a social evening. He did play a weekly game of cricket or hockey and, once in a while, hunted or sailed, but that was about all.

Andrews was steeped in shipbuilding for thirteen years, from the *Celtic* to the *Titanic*. During that time, he became assistant chief designer and then, at thirty-two, head of the designing department under Lord Pirrie. "One sees him, big and strong, a paint-smeared bowler hat on his crown, grease on his boots and the pockets of his blue jacket stuffed with plans, making his daily round of the Yards, now consulting his Chief, now conferring with a foreman, now interviewing an owner, now pouring over intricate calculations in the Drawing office."

Like Custer, Thomas Andrews was a strong man with a commanding physical presence. He stood a little under six feet, weighed two hundred pounds—most of that weight being in his upper body, his shoulders and his chest—and carried himself with an erect posture, military style. Like Custer, he was energetic and handsome—women noticed his sharp brown eyes. Custer bore a passion for his military career; Andrews harbored the same passion for building ships. Bullock mentions that Andrews was fond of Maeterlinck's *Life of the Bee*. Unlike Custer, however, Andrews was apparently universally admired. His friends and associates admired his unselfish nature and his love of humanity. And it was emblematic of Andrews that he and his wife should have printed on their Christmas card of 1910 a quote from Ruskin, "What we think, or what we know, or what we believe, is in the end of little consequence. The only thing of consequence is what we do."

At the moment the *Titanic* struck the iceberg, Andrews was reviewing the notes he had made during the first few days of the voyage. James Cameron's movie *Titanic* depicts Andrews drinking a glass of red wine over his worktable—for effect, the glass shakes during the seconds the iceberg strikes the hull—and yet it was unlikely that Andrews would have been drinking alcohol. Like Custer, he was a teetotaler. As a young man, he promised his parents to abstain even after he turned twenty-one.

In the time it took for Andrews to put his coat on, the bridge sprang into action. Captain Smith, First Officer Murdoch, and Fourth Officer Boxhall stepped out to the port wing and looked past the stern of the ship to see the last of the iceberg. Smith asked Boxhall to make a preliminary inspection of the ship, and the Fourth Officer dropped down to the steerage quarters beneath the forecastle head to discover the extent of the damage. He returned to the bridge to report that he had seen no damage.

Next, Smith asked Boxhall to find the ship's carpenter, John Hutchinson, to request that he sound the ship. Boxhall met the carpenter near the staircase leading to A Deck. "The ship is making water," said Hutchinson, who continued on up to the bridge. Boxhall made his way down to the mail hold where he found the clerks pulling mail from the racks while seawater swirled about their feet. When the Fourth Officer returned to the bridge and reported his news to Smith, the Captain turned away from him and said nothing. A few minutes later, as if to underscore with dreadful certainty Boxhall's report, the Captain noted that the ship's commutator already showed a list to starboard of five degrees.

Thomas Andrews pulled on his overcoat and, after conferring briefly with a huddle of first class passengers, made his way down to the womb of the ship. Above him, the other principal crewmen of the *Titanic* discovered the problem. Second Officer Lightoller, who had heard the jarring from his bunk, decided to remain in his quarters until another crewman—probably Boxhall—retrieved him. Chief Officer Henry Wilde, second-in-command, showed up at the bridge and asked Smith, "Is the damage serious?"

"Certainly," said the Captain. "I'm afraid it's more than serious."

Next on the bridge was the owner, Bruce Ismay, an overcoat over his pajamas.

"We have struck ice," Captain Smith told him.

"Do you think the ship is seriously damaged?"

"I'm afraid she is." This affectionate appeal to the ship's gender was a plaintive note before the epilogue. Nevertheless, the definitive answer on the ship's condition rested with the man who had built her.

Andrews made his careful inspection. He now knew that the first six compartments of the ship had been damaged. When the iceberg bumped

71

against the forward portion of the starboard hull, it punctured holes in the hull amounting to what sonar would later confirm was about twelve or thirteen square feet of actual damage. Yet Andrews knew the breach was distributed in such a way that it would be fatal. The *Titanic* could float with her first two or three or even four watertight compartments flooded. But her first five compartments were open to the sea, and a sixth was also damaged. Thus the ship's sinking was a mathematical certainty.

We can only guess what passed through Thomas Andrews' mind as he stared at the seawater pouring in through the damaged hull. Sixteen watertight compartments! And now six of them were damaged and the ship would founder! The technology had been available to make a ship that would have withstood this particular accident—an elongated side scraping of a ship—but Andrews and his superiors never imagined that their prized ship would strike an object that would do more damage than cracking open two watertight compartments at their conjunction. The principal technological flaw of the *Titanic* was that the watertight compartments were not sealed at their tops. As Andrews studied the seawater inside the ship, he realized that the water would fill the first three or four compartments. The weight of it would tip the bow down. Water would then fill the first compartment and spill into the second. The second would fill and spill over into the third. As the compartments filled, the bow of the ship would sink further and further into the sea. Had Andrews insisted on building the ship with a top bulkhead running the length of these compartments, the *Titanic* would have survived.

The technology to design a safe—and nearly unsinkable liner—existed at the time Andrews built the *Titanic*. As early as 1858, a ship called *The Great Eastern* had been built with watertight compartments and with additional longitudinal bulkheads creating what amounted to forty to fifty separate watertight compartments. Because these compartments were sealed from the entryway via a series of hatches, they were truly watertight. In addition, *The Great Eastern*, unlike the *Titanic*, was built with a double hull. Each hull was separated by nearly three feet of space and lined with supporting braces. In 1862, *The Great Eastern* had an accident similar to what happened to the *Titanic*. She struck an uncharted rock off Montauk Point, Long Island, that ripped an eighty-three foot gash in her starboard side (considering their size differences, a comparable injury to what befell the *Titanic*). But *The Great Eastern* survived—she sagged to starboard (her inner skin held) and traveled the rest of the way to New York under her own steam.

The problem for Andrews, however, was that the ship's ultimate design had been the call of the owners—Ismay and his managers. Perhaps he thought about this as he calculated the *Titanic's* doom that night. One could not design a ship that would be completely safe and yet arrive at the level of luxury that Ismay sought for the *Titanic*. A honeycomb of watertight compartments would have meant no grand staircase and no extra space for luxury suites for high-paying passengers. A double hull would have taken up valuable cargo space. Transverse bulkheads would have spoiled the effect of a spacious dining room.

Nevertheless, the fault of the *Titanic's* builder was not so much that he and others chose not to add all these safety features. Rather, it was that they lacked the vision to foresee an accident that would incur damage to more than two of the watertight compartments. This was a design failure, a failure of technology that would mirror some of the late-Twentieth Century's more acute airline disasters.

IX

INVESTIGATORS NEVER FULLY SOLVED THE CASE of USAir Flight 427, but findings suggest design problems similar to those that caused the *Titanic* to sink. Thomas Haueter, one of the senior investigators of the National Transportation Safety Board, spent months studying Flight 427, and through a battery of sophisticated tests, discovered a series of mechanical events that caused the plane to roll uncontrollably. Twenty-six seconds before impact, the pilots realized that ordinary efforts at flight and recovery would not avail. Flight 427 had a sudden burst in airspeed, from 190 knots up to and over 195 knots and then, a second later, back down to 190 knots again. Tests also revealed that the plane's heading had changed by two degrees, nose to the left, three seconds after the speed burst and then another six degrees to the left a moment after that. The plane went into a yawing movement in which the tail had swung to the right while the nose had swung left, giving the impression that the plane had skidded in the air.

Yaws are nearly always induced by movement of the rudder, the large vertical panel in the tail. Unlike ships at sea, rudders on aircraft are seldom used; pilots turn the planes with gentle banking movements by means of control panels on the wings. In the case of Flight 427, as the plane's nose pivoted left, the right wing had moved swiftly through the air. This sharp movement had given the right wing lift, which, in turn, forced the left wing down. Within eight seconds, the left wing had come down to over a sixty-degree angle and then moments later to 138 degrees while the pitch downward was eighty-six degrees, only a few degrees short of vertical. By then, the crash of Flight 427 was inevitable.

In the case of the *Titanic*, ice punctured the hull and water flooded into the ship. The weight of the water caused the bow to tip downward. The lack of sealed bulkheads allowed the water to flow over the top of each compartment, thus sinking the ship. Flight 427 experienced a rare hard-over movement of its rudder causing the plane to yaw. This yaw caused lift of the right wing and an ensuing roll that the pilots were unable to control. Ships designed after the *Titanic* sealed the watertight compartments at their tops. Now, partly because of Flight 427 and similar problems with other 737s, Boeing's new fleet comes equipped with better rudder control mechanisms.

Both the disasters of Flight 427 and the *Titanic* reveal the designers' inability to foresee the fatal circumstances that would bring about disaster. Unfortunately, the later Twentieth Century and now the Twenty-First Century have presented us with artificial systems and circumstances more and more complex—so complex, in fact, that one wonders if we will ever properly design our machines.

In his book, *Inside the Sky: A Meditation on Flight*, William Langewiesche argues that there are three kinds of transportation failures: procedural failures, engineered failures, and system failures. Procedural failures arise from human error. For example, in the Azores in 1983, a KLM pilot decided to take off without proper clearance from the tower and crashed his Boeing 747 into a Pan Am 747 sitting on the fog-bound runway before him. In other words, the pilot did not follow the proper procedure.

Engineered failures result from equipment or design failures. One classic example: an American Eagle ATR turboprop crashed in Indiana in 1974 because de-icing boots did not protect its wings from freezing rain. The crash of Flight 427 was an engineered failure.

The most problematic of the three is system failure. Although the *Titanic* disaster bore elements of an engineered failure, it would be better to characterize the accident as a system failure. The crash of ValuJet Flight 592 provides insight into the kind of system failure that doomed the *Titanic*. Langewieshe describes the unusual circumstances that brought down this airplane.

In May 1996, ValuJet was expanding rapidly. Like the White Star Line, ValuJet wanted to accommodate more and more passengers. To that end, ValuJet had purchased three MD-80s and began refurbishing them at one of their hangars in Miami. To do this job, the company had contracted with SabreTech, which, in turn, hired contract mechanics on an as-needed basis—in essence, a crew of temporary workers. ValuJet told SabreTech to replace the oxygen generators on the MD-80s.

Oxygen generators are used on board an aircraft to induce the flow of oxygen to the oxygen masks that drop in front of each passenger if the cabin loses pressure. To activate the flow of oxygen, each passenger pulls a lanyard which, in turn, pulls a retaining pin free from a spring-loaded hammer. This hammer falls on a mini-explosive charge that sparks a chemical reaction that frees oxygen within the sodium-chlorate core. This reaction produces a heat-surface temperature on a canister that may rise to five hundred degrees Fahrenheit which, under the worst scenarios, makes these oxygen generators veritable firebombs if not handled properly.

At any rate, ValuJet told its contractor, SabreTech, to replace these oxygen generators because they had reached the end of their recommended lifetimes. ValuJet gave SabreTech explicit instructions on how the generators were to be removed and handled. SabreTech workers removed the generators, taped or cut each of their lanyards, and placed them into five cardboard boxes they found in the ValuJet hangar. These workers believed that securing the lanyards would prevent an inadvertent firing of any of the generators. Unfortunately, the workers neglected to place required plastic safety caps over the firing pins—a point clearly stated in ValuJet's work order. None of the SabreTech workers had access to these safety caps and likely felt that it was an unnecessary precaution, much like extra lifeboats on a ship with a reputation for being unsinkable.

SabreTech's contract workers, in a rush to get the job done for an impatient ValuJet, signed off on the form requiring installation of the safety caps. Supervisors reviewed the paperwork, but did not bother to ask whether the work had actually been done. The five boxes then sat for a few weeks in a parts rack beside the airplanes before being moved to SabreTech's shipping and receiving department where they sat in an area designated as ValuJet property. A SabreTech manager ordered his shipping clerk to clean up the area in preparation for an inspection by Continental Airlines, a potential SabreTech customer. The shipping clerk prepared to send the boxes—still unmarked— back to ValuJet headquarters in Atlanta by making sure the canisters were packed tightly, sealing each box, addressing each with ValuJet information, and writing in "aircraft parts" as a description of the contents.

Next, in preparation for shipment, he asked the receiving clerk to make out a shipping ticket with the description "oxygen canisters—empty" on the shipping form. In addition to the five boxes, the shipment included two ValuJet main tires and a smaller nose tire. On May 11, a SabreTech driver finally brought the boxes and tires—as instructed—to Flight 592, a ValuJet DC-9 bound for Atlanta. The ValuJet ramp agent accepted the boxes even though he was forbidden to do so by federal regulations that prohibit transporting used canisters because their discharge contains toxic residue. ValuJet was not licensed to carry any such hazardous materials. The ramp agent even discussed this cargo with the flight's co-pilot, Richard Hazen. The two of them decided to place the five boxes and three tires in the forward hold in a rather unstable arrangement. Therefore, as Flight 592 prepared for takeoff, its cargo hold contained a volatile mixture of rubber tires, cardboard, and ignitable oxygen canisters.

In a system failure, the accident is caused by the very functioning of the system or industry within which the accident occurred. In this particular system, there were so many elements linked in multiple and often unpredictable ways, that their unforeseeable combinations caused, in turn, the failure of other parts. Since the system was large, the combination of failures multiplied. In this case, ValuJet was expanding too rapidly (from two to fifty-two planes in just two-and-a-half years), and possessed neither the rules nor the personnel to ensure adequate safety procedures. In addition, the FAA was busy fighting terrorism and could assign only three inspectors to the airline. Even with this low level of inspections, the company was found guilty of a disproportionate number of safety infractions. An aircraft maintenance group, alarmed by these infractions, as well as by the FAA's casual attitude toward ValuJet, recommended that ValuJet should be de-certified—in essence, grounded—immediately. This recommendation was sent to Washington but lay buried in a mountain of paperwork until after the accident.

Because ValuJet was pushing SabreTech to get the three MD-80s refurbished as soon as possible, six hundred people worked on the project and many of those logged overtime. These men and women, some of whom spoke very little English, were expected to understand the distinction in ValuJet's written safety procedures between oxygen canisters that were "expired" and oxygen canisters that were "not expended." The latter required the plastic safety caps that no one could seem to find. Where could they turn for advice? Even for those who could read English, the MD-80 maintenance manual was of little help. Chapter 35-22-01 states that "all serviceable and unserviceable [unexpended] oxygen generators [canisters] are to be stored in an area that ensures that each unit is not exposed to high temperatures or possible damage." The manual also includes this admonition: "An expended oxygen generator [canister] contains both barium oxide and asbestos fibers and must be disposed of in accordance with local regulatory compliances and using authorized procedures."

These confusions were compounded by the relationship between the airlines and the Federal Aviation Administration. The FAA was overbooked and focused on terrorism. Just as critically, the FAA had been assigned a dual mandate by Congress to promote the airline industry as well as regulate it. The day after Flight 592 went down, the head of FAA, David Hinson, flew to Miami and declared to the press that ValuJet was a safe airline—a statement even more preposterous than that made by the White Star Line official who in New York said that under no circumstances could the great ship sink, even after his technical people had failed to raise the ship's captain for nearly five hours. Hinson's statement that ValuJet was a safe airline arose from the close relationship between the FAA and the airlines it is supposed to regulate.

Each airline wants to compete fairly with other firms. So top executives work hand-in-hand with the FAA to ensure that the competition is equally regulated. In this way, the airlines actually need the FAA. The FAA, in turn, has sought to work carefully and closely with the leaders of an intensely competitive industry—in effect, to appease and promote their companies.

X

A SIMILAR SITUATION EXISTED WITH THE TITANIC. The British Board of Trade—the regulatory body that oversaw safety and other regulations for the passenger liners in 1912—had a cozy relationship with the owners of the shipping companies. When Thomas Andrews made his inspection of the ship and saw that the damage done would be fatal, he must have known that the ship carried lifeboats for only 1,178 of the 2,201 souls on board. He had built this ship according to instructions—and here he was, faced with this disaster. Lack of lifeboats? The decision to limit the number of lifeboats is mired in complexity. Walter Lord's second book on the subject gives a good picture of how the Board of Trade, like the FAA, failed in some key areas.

First, the shipping business—like the deregulated airline industry seventy years later—was growing rapidly. Rules governing the number of lifeboats on board a vessel dated to 1894 and had not been revised. Second, the number of lifeboats per ship was based on the cubic space of each ship rather than on the number of people for which the ship was built. Third, members of the Board of Trade deferred in a roundabout way to the owners whose ships they were supposed to regulate. Why was this? Primarily because the Board of Trade members knew relatively little about the details of modern shipping and ships at sea. An exception was Alexander Carlisle, managing director of Harland & Wolff in 1909 while the *Titanic* was being built. He proposed equipping the *Titanic* with at least forty-eight lifeboats instead of twenty, but his plan was scuttled by the owners of the line (including Ismay). Carlisle himself never pressed his recommendation. Years later when asked why, he delivered a remarkably honest and business-like answer. Requiring the *Titanic* to have "lifeboats for all" would have put the rest of the White Star fleet in an awkward position. At any rate, the *Titanic* was in full compliance with existing regulations on both sides of the Atlantic—a fact that Ismay pointed out when questioned on the subject by US Senator Francis Newlands of Nevada during the 1912 Senate Investigation.

Senator Newlands asked, "What was the full equipment of lifeboats for a ship of this size?"

Ismay replied, "I could not tell you that, sir. That is covered by the Board of Trade regulations. She may have exceeded the Board of Trade regulations, for all I know. I could not answer that question. Anyhow, she had sufficient boats to obtain her passenger certificate, and therefore she must have been fully boated, according to the requirements of the English Board of Trade, which I understand are accepted by this country."

Thomas Andrews had built the *Titanic* according to the specifications handed down by the brass of the White Star Line, including Ismay, and yet Andrews, unfortunately, was not in a position to have the final word on all the details. As he made his way to the bridge to deliver his news to the Captain—news that would be the final word on the ship's fate—he likely saw with irony a host of calm passengers and calm crewmen. The strange serenity of a ship sinking very slowly on a windless sea contrasts sharply with the circumstances of late-Twentieth Century air disasters. In the case of Flight 592, passengers knew right away that something was wrong when they saw smoke creeping into the cabin.

Flight 592 left Miami for Atlanta at around 2:00 PM, piloted by thirty-five-year-old Caralyn Kubeck. Kubeck had nine thousand flight hours under her belt, two thousand of them on DC-9s. The flight was co-piloted by fifty-two-year-old Richard Hazen, an ex-Air Force pilot. Six minutes into the flight, while the plane climbed to eleven thousand feet, Kubeck noted a pulse of high pressure—perhaps a tire exploding—which sounded like a chirp and a simultaneous beep on the public address system.

"What was that?" she asked her co-pilot.

"I don't know," said Hazen.

Kubeck's first thought was that the plane had some electrical malfunction that had caused the circuit breakers to switch over.

Hazen said, "Yeah, that battery charger's kicking in."

Then Kubeck. "We're losing everything. We need, we need to get back to Miami."

Before either crewmember had the chance to radio the tower, they heard shouting from the passenger cabin and then the word "fire." At that point, Hazen radioed the Miami controller, "Ah, five-ninety-two needs an immediate return to Miami."

The Miami controller was Jesse Fisher, thirty-six, with seven years experience. In his dialogue with Hazen, he referred to the plane as "Critter" because of the ValuJet logo of a smiley face on the front of the airplane. Now, with absolutely clear weather, he radioed back to Hazen, "Critter five-ninety-two, ah roger, turn left heading two-seven-zero, descend and maintain seven thousand." Hazen acknowledged the command. So far, so good. Now the controller took a moment to inquire, "What kind of problem are you having?"

The reply was firm, urgent. "Ah, smoke in the cockpit. Smoke in the cabin."

Jesse Fisher, of course, did not know that flammable oxygen canisters had been placed in the forward cargo hold and were surrounded by cardboard, which, in turn, was surrounded by rubber tires. All he knew was that the plane on his radar screen was in serious trouble. He said over his shoulder, "I need a supervisor here!" Then he said to the plane, "Critter five-ninety-two, you are cleared to descend to five thousand."

By now, the supervisor had plugged in beside Fisher. Inside the plane, the cockpit door once again opened and the voice of the chief flight attendant could be heard saying, "Okay, we need oxygen. We can't get oxygen back there." Flight 592 had not yet started to turn. Fisher's next transmission to Hazen was garbled. "Critter five-ninety-two, they're going to be standing, standing by for you. You can plan Runway One-two. When able, direct to Dolphin now."

Hazen interrupted, "Need radar vectors." His transmission was garbled by loud background noises. Fisher replied, "Critter five-ninety-two, turn left heading one-four-zero."

Hazen acknowledged, "One-four-zero." Finally, the flight began a gradual left turn and descended.

"Critter five-ninety-two, contact Miami Approach on—correction, no, you keep on my frequency."

No response.

On the screen Fisher watched the plane turn and then enter into a steep dive beginning at about 750 feet. It appeared that the pilots had lost control of the aircraft. Clearly, the fire on the plane was a serious one—probably the cockpit and cabin were filled with black smoke. Then Flight 592 rolled to a sixty-five degree left bank and dove 6,400 feet in thirty-two seconds. As Fisher watched the plane's steep dive, he radioed, "Critter five-ninety-two, you can, ah, turn left, heading one-zero-zero, and join the Runway One-two localizer at Miami . . . Critter five-ninety-two, descend and maintain three thousand." Suddenly the plane pulled up from its dive and flew level at an altitude of about a thousand feet. Perhaps, by some miracle, the smoke had cleared from the cockpit enough to allow either pilot to regain control of the aircraft. "Critter five-ninety-two, Opa-locka Airport's about ah twelve o'clock at fifteen miles." It had finally dawned on Fisher that Flight 592 was too badly damaged to return to Miami, but by then any airport was too far away. A fisherman named Walton Little standing in his bass boat in the Florida Everglades saw the plane roll steeply and nose dive into the ground at a speed later determined to be about five hundred miles-an-hour.

XI

ON BOARD THE TITANIC, THE LACK OF SPEED and the failure of engine vibration were what her passengers and crew most noticed. In his succinct account, second class passenger Lawrence Beezley noted the sudden cessation of the ship's engines. That silence was a jarring, unsettling absence of sound. But it was Thomas Andrews who, along with the Captain, felt responsibility for the ship and its passengers.

As his biographer reports, Andrews was a knowledgable figure to whom the first class passengers looked for clues as to what might happen to the *Titanic*. "At first we did not realize," said Mr. Albert Dick, "that the Titanic was mortally wounded . . . I do not believe that anyone on her realized she was going to sink . . . Mr. Andrews was on hand at once and said that he was going below to investigate. We begged him not to go, but he insisted, saying he knew the ship as no one else did and that he might be able to allay the fears of the passengers. He went. As the minutes flew by we did not know what to do or which way to turn. But in the midst of most of us there was the feeling that something was going to happen, and we waited for Mr. Andrews to come back. When finally he came we hung upon his words, and they were these, 'There is no cause for any excitement. All of you get what you can in the way of clothes and come on deck as soon as you can. She is torn to bits below, but she will not sink if her bulkheads hold.'"

Of course, Andrews knew better than anyone that the ship was doomed. His words to Mr. Albert Dick and others were meant to prevent panic. A woman from Portland, Oregon, Mrs. Frank M. Warren, remembered seeing Andrews at the foot of the grand staircase on D Deck as he made his way upward toward the bridge. When asked if there was any danger, he made no reply. Mrs. Warren did not get a close look at Andrews, but a passenger who was later saved said that his face was terribly troubled.

Seventeen-year-old Jack Thayer, a first class passenger, survived the sinking ship by jumping into the water and swimming to an overturned lifeboat, but the experience of the *Titanic* never left him. Of life before the disaster, he wrote, "There was peace and the world had an even tenor to its ways. . . . In those days one could freely circulate around the world, in both a physical and an economic sense, and definitely plan for the future. . . . True enough, from time to time there were events—catastrophes—like the Johnstown Flood, the San Francisco Earthquake, or floods in China—which stirred the sleeping world, but not enough to keep it from resuming its slumber. It seems to me that the disaster about to occur was the event that not only made the world rub its eyes and awake, but woke it with a start, keeping it moving at a rapidly accelerating pace ever since, with less and less peace, satisfaction, and happiness." Thayer, an introspective man, took his own life in 1945 when he learned that his son had been killed in World War Two.

After making his midnight inspection of the damaged hull, Thomas Andrews, for the moment, kept the exact nature of the ship's wound to himself. And for good reason. Once he told the Captain of the damage, he would have an hour, maybe more, to assist passengers into the lifeboats. Perhaps, after the last lifeboat had been lowered, he would reflect on how decades of work, and the faith of those who believed in the evolution of science and technology, would founder with this ship. He hadn't been below long. From the railing, Andrews beheld a panoply of stars. He climbed the steps to the lighted passageway outside the bridge where the Captain was waiting for him.

As late as 2:10 AM, ten minutes before the ship would sink, an assistant

THE LAST MAN OF THE NINETEENTH CENTURY

I

IN JUNE 1914, EDWARD GREY LEARNED that his eyesight was failing. His doctor predicted that he would lose his ability to read unless he wore dark glasses as often as possible and worked far fewer hours.

An athletic, handsome man of fifty-two with a distinctive Roman nose, Grey took the news of his failing eyesight hard. He was a tireless worker. He was also a reclusive man who loved the outdoors. Losing his eyesight would mean he'd be forced to give up his beloved squash games, although he could still spend time along the rivers he loved. Grey had written a book on fly-fishing that was well respected by anglers. He once told a friend that, even if he were to lose his eyesight entirely, he could still fish his favorite pools using only his memory.

In June 1914, Edward Grey was Britain's foreign secretary—and had been for nine years. These were years when he worked patiently to maintain peace in Europe by cultivating careful alliances with other European powers, particularly France. The summer of 1914 was unusually sunny and serene. The calm was deceptive, however. Europe was a tinderbox where the slightest spark could bring about a general and disastrous war.

The principal problem, as Grey saw it, was Germany. Or, more precisely, German hegemony and Germany's alliance with the Austro-Hungarian Empire. Both Germany and Austria sought ways to expand their influence in continental Europe. And each was surrounded by mistrustful neighbors. Austria wanted to quell Serbia's growing desire to form a Southern Slav

Kingdom that, along with Montenegro, might spur Austria's Slavic subjects to break away from the Empire. Germany would probably back Austria in a war with Serbia.

On the other side, Russia saw herself as the major Slav power, and any Austrian action against Serbia might bring Russia into the battle on the side of the Serbs. If Russia and Germany fought, France would likely choose to honor its treaty with Russia by declaring war against Germany. If Germany sensed that France (Germany's traditional enemy) wanted a war, Germany might well invade France through Belgium. If Germany attacked France, Britain could decide to enter the war on the French side. Although Britain did not have a formal treaty with France (the two countries maintained an *entente,* or an informal agreement to cooperate), Britain *did* have a formal treaty with Belgium. A violation of Belgian neutrality would almost certainly bring Britain into war.

Throughout his career, Grey had always distrusted the Germans. As early as 1903, in a private letter to a friend, Grey wrote that he had "come to think that Germany is our worst enemy and our greatest danger. I do not doubt that there are many Germans well disposed to us, but they are a minority; and the majority dislike us so intensely that the friendship of their Emperor or their Government cannot be really useful to us."

Edward Grey was born in 1862 into a distinguished family from Northumberland in the northeast corner of England near the Scottish border. He was blessed with a famous ancestor, Earl Grey, the tea man. The Grey family inhabited an historical family estate called Fallodon, an enormous country house two miles from the North Sea which young Edward could view from the east garden through a gap in the trees. Edward's grandfather was Sir George Grey, British home secretary in 1846. Edward's father, Colonel George Henry Grey, was a career army man who became ill and died at thirty-nine.

Edward was twelve when his father died. He was the oldest of seven children and was expected to step into his father's shoes, to uphold family honor, to "make something" of himself. Nevertheless, Grey did poorly in his studies at Oxford and, in January 1884, was reprimanded. The next two months were pivotal. "When I was sent down from Oxford I lived the months of February and March entirely alone but I was never dull. I bought my first five pairs of waterfowl, which afterwards became a great interest in my life . . ."

Fourteen years later, Grey reflected on his Oxford period in a letter to a friend:

So you read *The Times* hungrily from cover to cover! You are so much more suited to be a Cabinet Minister than I am. I am now as I was when I read for some Oxford examination in the Vicarage garden at Embleton, and got restless when I saw the gardener wheeling the wheelbarrow outside, and wanted to change my work for his having 'all my young affections out of doors.' Someday when there is a storm and you are all hugging your houses and reading your *Timeses,* I shall take the road and be no more seen and wander till I cease upon the midnight somewhere in the open air. The life I led at Oxford was one of pure pleasure and of a kind that I could not have enjoyed at any other time of life. It led to nothing, but it left no scars, nothing to be regretted or effaced. It cleared the way for serious things.

Indeed, it did clear the way for serious things. Later that spring, Grey took the time to properly prepare for his examinations. That summer he won an undistinguished degree in jurisprudence from Oxford. He was a different man now—his ambitionless days were over. He decided to go into politics. Through a family connection, he found a job as private secretary to Sir Evelyn Baring, who stayed in London for an Egyptian conference during the summer and early autumn of 1884. In October, Grey began working for the Treasury, a job he held until he decided to run for Parliament the following summer.

Grey's campaign, however, was interrupted by romance. Grey fell in love with a Northumberland squire's daughter named Dorothy Widdington, and they were married in October 1885. The next month Grey won a seat in the House of Commons at the unusually young age of twenty-three. Over the previous eighteen months—since his Oxford reprimand and his two months in the country—a sense of purpose had arisen within his Nineteenth Century soul. He embraced the twin virtues of intellectual reflection and public duty.

Edward Grey was beloved by his constituents in Northumberland and won re-election repeatedly. As the years passed, he rose within the Liberal party because of his vision and abilities as well as his friendship with Herbert Asquith (who would become prime minister) and with Richard Haldane (who would become head of the War Office).

Edward Grey loved good food and wine. In addition to squash, Grey was an avid tennis player who once won a national amateur title. In 1902, at forty, Grey had nearly seventeen years of parliamentary experience behind him. He was respected by his colleagues and had emerged as a thoughtful national figure. He was in the prime of life.

Like George Custer and Thomas Andrews, Grey was deeply in love with his wife. Every April they opened a cottage they had purchased on the River Itchen in Hampshire not far from London. During the long parliamentary sessions, Edward and Dorothy walked to the Waterloo station early Saturday mornings before there was any traffic about, boarded a train, and arrived at the cottage by eight to have breakfast. Each Monday morning they returned reluctantly to London, to what Dorothy described as "the blackness of town life, with its unworthy aims, mistakes, and general devilishness."

Grey echoed Dorothy's sentiments. He felt most at home in this cottage, even though Fallodon, the family estate in Northumberland, was a close second. But Grey felt obliged to return to London. It was the big city where great decisions were made, but the climate was unpleasant, particularly in the summer. "There is an aspect of London which is inevitable and becomes most oppressive in hot June days," he wrote. "There is the aggressive stiffness of the buildings, the brutal hardness of the pavement, the smell of the streets festering in the sun, the glare of the light all day striking upon hard substances, and the stuffiness of the heat from which there is no relief at night—for no coolness comes with the evening air, and bedroom and windows seem to open into ovens."

When the Liberal party entered a difficult and intense period in the early part of the century, Grey complained that all the time he spent on politics had ruined his opportunity to savor the roses and honeysuckle surrounding his cottage. On the River Itchen, he and his wife fished for trout together, took long walks, watched for birds, and admired flowers. Edward and Dorothy would not allow visitors to discuss politics. In late June, they closed the cottage and departed north to the windswept heath of Fallodon and its clear ocean views.

The hustle and bustle of London was difficult for the Greys. And they feared that London presaged a future of machines and cities, an age of factories, smokestacks, trains, and motor cars. "My wife and I are still not sure that we quite welcome the prospect of the Twentieth Century," Grey wrote. He divided his time between the evil of urban life and the good of nature. Urban life included the difficult world of politics, and during these years political events were troubling. In April 1909, he wrote to a friend, "My holiday was wrecked by Constantinople & Persia: I made an attempt to salmon fish & had two days of it at Rosehall and one Sunday on which I walked up a lonely glen amongst many pairs of curlews & heard ravens & lunched by a burn in the sun. Then I had to decide to return to London just as the fishing was at its very best. I do long to be free to enjoy country life again."

Edward Grey dreaded German militarism. From his position at the Foreign Office, he knew that the Germans were preparing plans for the next war. He knew that in Berlin, a thin, monocled Prussian officer named Count Alfred von Schlieffen had taken the position of chief of the German general staff. A tall, lean man, with a narrow, aristocratic face, Schlieffen worked in his crisp army uniform and operated under the motto, "Be bold, be bold." Grey knew that Schlieffen planned for German expansion and conquest, and that he did so with such single-mindedness and attention to detail that little else concerned him. Grey was aware that the Schlieffen Plan was formed from decades of Prussian military thinking and was the natural next step to Clausewitz's call for quick victory through decisive action. Grey could only guess at the specifics of the plan, but the outlines were clear to any observer. Decisive battle meant smashing and liquidating the enemy's forces. Such a result could only come by a flank rather than a frontal attack, or, better yet, through double envelopment—two simultaneous flank attacks—the maneuver that all military historians admired, the tactic used by Hannibal at the Battle of Cannae to defeat the Romans.

Just how good was the Schlieffen Plan? Good enough that, in 1940, Adolph Hitler would use a revised Schlieffen Plan to achieve a double envelopment. Hitler overran Belgium, the Netherlands, Luxembourg, and France in just three weeks time by attacking western Europe with one set of divisions via the low countries, while other divisions stealthily penetrated northern France through the Ardennes Forest. Hitler avoided France's much heralded Maginot Line and achieved a stunning victory. "The great battle of France is over," wrote a young German officer in 1940. "It lasted twenty-six years."

Alfred von Schlieffen believed that France and Russia were bound to join any conflict as Germany's enemies. He predicted that Russia would take nearly six weeks to mobilize after the outbreak of war. So he decided to commit most of Germany's forces against France, the stronger enemy, before turning back to fight Russia on a second front. Schlieffen's plan grew larger with each successive year. By 1905 it called for an enveloping right-wing sweep in which the German armies would cross Belgium from Liege to Brussels before turning southward where they could take advantage of the open country of Flanders to knife into France. Victory against France depended upon speed.

Schlieffen planned war; Edward Grey planned peace. Grey spent the first years of the new century formulating a plan for Europe that he hoped would maintain peace by balancing the power of one nation against another. Schlieffen grounded his war plans in his reading of von Clausewitz. Edward Grey grounded his peace plans in his reading of Wordsworth. Grey developed a strong interior life founded on a sense of God in nature and an unyielding abhorrence of war. He believed wholeheartedly that man's greatest joy— and his highest aspiration—was participating in the workings of nature. He found in Wordsworth's writings the poetic articulations of his own inner life.

Wordsworth *felt* strongly and intensely. He gave to his readers the assurance that moral choices were significant events in the universe, and that human life was always surrounded and supported by immense forces. Committees and parliamentary dealings, by comparison, were trivial. Grey believed this, too, and the difficulty of his life was to keep his public and private worlds in balance. He worried constantly about the damage that Liberal party policies might do to the land. Moreover, it caused him great pain that Europe was turning into a man-made world of sprawling cities and a vulgarized countryside. War was the ultimate horror to him—and especially the kind of all-out war that would be fought in the Twentieth Century, war that was the product of the machine mind.

The foremost object of Grey's career was to avoid war. Schlieffen, in contrast, thought of little else but launching and executing war. As each year passed, Schlieffen made more and more refinements to his plan, enhancing its central element, "a heavily one-sided right wing that would spread across the whole of Belgium on both sides of the Meuse, sweep down through the country like a monstrous hay rake, cross the Franco-Belgian frontier along its entire width, and descend upon Paris along the Valley of Oise."

Everything depended upon a strong right wing. Schlieffen wanted these divisions to reach as far west as the town of Lille to ensure complete entrapment of the French. "When you march into France," he said, "let the last man on the right brush the Channel with his sleeve." Of course, Schlieffen also expected the French to marshal their forces in an attempt to regain the provinces of Alsace and Lorraine that they had lost to the Germans in the war of 1870. Schlieffen envisioned that the German left wing could hold the French forces in their center until the right wing could complete its sweeping envelopment. "A victory on the battlefield is of little account," he said, "if it has not resulted either in breakthrough or encirclement."

Thus, the French army would be surrounded and annihilated in a move straight from the text of von Clausewitz.

The German High Command frequently used such words as *vernichten* (annihilate), *liquidieren* (liquidate), *zerschmettern* (smash), and *zerstoren* (destroy). Schlieffen wanted to win and win quickly. Having embraced the strategy of decisive battle, Schlieffen pinned Germany's fate to it. He expected France to cross Belgium's frontier in its plan to recapture their lost provinces. Why not beat them to the punch? Germany would cross the border first.

One of Schlieffen's assumptions was that Belgium would not fight. Skeptics in the German High Command attacked Schlieffen's plan in 1904, citing Bismarck's warning that it would be against "plain common sense" to add Belgium to the forces against Germany. Two years later, at age seventy-three, Schlieffen retired from military planning to devote full-time to answering his critics. He lobbied hard for the principles of his scheme: a double envelopment inspired by Hannibal at the Battle of Cannae. Schlieffen lived to eighty and died in 1913, a year before the outbreak of war. As he lay on his deathbed in his home in Berlin, he uttered a last piece of advice. "It must come to a fight," he said. "For God's sake, make the right wing strong."

Grey did what he could to counter Germany's war plans. His friend in the War Office, Richard Haldane, fed him information gleaned from intelligence dispatches. Even though both Grey and Haldane were worried about the cost of planning for war, each felt that Britain's army had to be ready to serve overseas, and they agreed that the answer could not be a large force of conscripts due to the time it would take to train them. The emphasis had to be on mobility and efficiency. Britain would make up in quality what it lacked in quantity. By July 1906, Grey and Haldane were ready with plans for an expeditionary force of 150,000 men with specialist groups.

But the year 1906 also brought to Edward Grey a personal loss harsher than anything the Germans could concoct. On February 1, Grey had just finished lunch and was meeting with the defense committee when his private secretary brought him a telegram: his wife, Dorothy, was lying unconscious in a schoolhouse near Fallodon.

That morning, Dorothy had gone for a carriage ride along the lanes north of the estate. The head groom warned her that the horse was in an agitated state and might bolt, but she had insisted. Sure enough, the horse shied and Dorothy was thrown from the carriage. Grey caught the evening train and arrived after midnight. He sensed at once that the situation was grave. That following morning he wrote to Haldane that Dorothy's chances of survival were slim, for she had a fracture at the base of her skull. As it was, her prolonged unconsciousness caused Grey a deepening dread. Three days later, early in the morning, she died.

This was the second death to strike Grey within a year. Seven months earlier, his mother had died of an illness from which she had been expected to recover. "The death of Mother," he wrote, "brings mortality home to me more than anything I have known. It is like a landslide in my past."

Grey was alone now, and he spent the first months after Dorothy's death fighting his loneliness. "This week is worse than last week; the cold & weight of the separation are more felt . . . I feel like a prisoner in a cell who beats his head against the walls; but these fits pass or cease at any rate while I do my work." Previously, he carefully paced himself and kept his political life and personal life in strict balance. Now, to blunt the pain of Dorothy's death, he threw himself into his work.

Grey's work was of the greatest importance—he was attempting to prevent war. During the next eight years, leading up to 1914, Grey remained determined to stand by the French *entente* as a way to keep Germany in check. In his memoirs, Grey denied making use of the term "balance of power." He nevertheless saw the European situation in these terms. On one side stood Germany and her ally, the Austro-Hungarian Empire. On the other side stood France and Russia. It was a face-off, a balance of power. And Britain was the wild card. "The Germans do not realize," said Grey, "that England has always drifted or deliberately gone into opposition to any power which establishes a hegemony in Europe."

II

IN 1914 THE BALANCE OF POWER WAS STRUCK A SHIFTING and ultimately deadly blow. The Austrians had long been resented by Serbs and other Slavs to the south. The Austrians occupied the provinces of Bosnia and Hercegovina whose residents were primarily Serbian. Yet the Austrians did not occupy nearby Serbia with its capital in Belgrade. Nevertheless, most Serbs longed to overthrow the Austrians and to join a Greater Serbia. They looked for any chance to strike at the Austrians. And now, on June 28, the Austrian Archduke and heir to the throne was assassinated in Sarajevo by a nineteen-year-old Bosnian Serb named Gavrilo Princip.

The Austrian Archduke was named Franz Ferdinand. His wife, Sophie, was from Bohemia (now part of the Czech Republic) and certainly far below the pedigree expected of a wife to the would-be emperor. Franz Ferdinand and his wife were admired by many Austrians, yet they had their detractors. Chief among them was Franz Josef, the current emperor of Austria-Hungary, and Franz Ferdinand's uncle. Franz Josef was a tall, bald man with mutton chop whiskers who lived in Vienna, rising early every morning and devoting himself almost obsessively to affairs of state. He disliked his nephew, Ferdinand, and disapproved of his marriage. In fact, he tried to stop the union, believing that to follow the traditions of the monarchy one must marry appropriately. But Franz Ferdinand would not hear of an arranged marriage. "If some member of our family is attracted to someone," he once commented, "there is always some slight blemish in her ancestry which rules out marriage. So we constantly marry our relatives and the result is that of the children of these unions half are cretins or epileptics."

Franz Ferdinand believed he would make a point to his uncle by visiting Sarajevo on June 28, his fourteenth wedding anniversary. He was not frightened at the prospect of an assassination, for he was both a courageous and foolhardy man who believed in fate. Speaking earlier of the members of his royal family, he said, "We are all constantly in danger of death. One must simply trust in God." A few years before, when a Portuguese aristocrat was assassinated by one of his subjects, Franz Ferdinand observed, "They are shooting us like sparrows from the rooftops."

Of course, one wonders whether Franz Ferdinand understood the significance of the date of his visit for the local Serbs. Did he know that June 28 was the day of St. Vitus, a patron saint of Serbia? Did he know that, on this day in 1389, the Ottoman Turks destroyed the last army of the Serbs at the battle of Kosov Field? Even though the Serbs lost this battle, generations remembered the heroic deed accomplished the night of June 28. After the battle, a Serbian nobleman named Milos Obilic crept into the tent of the victorious Turkish leader, stabbed the sultan to death, and was then hacked to death by the sultan's guards. The battle of Kosov Field on June 28 and the deed of Milos Obilic were legendary to the Serbs.

Gavrilo Princip and his fellow Serb conspirators thought deeply about the history of their people. Born in 1894 to a poor family in the western mountains of Bosnia, Princip was called Gavrilo because he was born on St. Gabriel's day, July 13. Princip and his family were Christian peasants known as kmets, who, typically, were oppressed by their Muslim landlords.

An English traveler in 1875 noted that the *kmet* in this area, "is worse off than many a serf in our darkest ages, and lies as completely at the mercy of the Mahometan [Muslim] owner of the soil as if he were a slave."

The Austrians were of no help when they took over Bosnia. Faced with the alternative of winning over these Christian Serbian peasants by emancipating them, or retaining the existing feudal system with the support of the Muslim landowners, they chose the latter. The historian Edmond Taylor remarks that the Muslims in Bosnia "are paradoxically the only friends the Catholic Habsburgs have in this seething, semi-Oriental province only recently freed from the Turkish yoke." As it was, the Muslim landowners would not agree to agrarian reform even if the Austrians had pushed the point. To emancipate Princip's family and other Christian peasants would ruin the Muslims financially. So the *kmets* in these western mountains, in harsh conditions, toiled on without hope.

Princip's family came from the most remote of these mountains called the Krajina in northwest Bosnia, the scene of bitter fighting during the insurrection of 1875-1877. The hardship and violence of the region was captured in Serb folksong:

> Krajina's like a blood-soaked rag;
> Blood is our fare at noon, blood still at evening,
> On every lip is the taste of blood,
> With never a peaceful day or any rest.

The Krajina Mountains where the Princip family lived were bordered on the west by the Dinaric Alps that rose to six thousand feet and separated Bosnia from Dalmatia and the Adriatic Sea. The mountains consisted of highlands split by valleys a few miles long and covered with red earth. At the end of long and bitterly cold winters, the valleys were irrigated by melting snow. Princip and his kinsmen lived in small villages dotting the valleys and mountainside. They huddled together in their misery, scratching out a bare existence.

Princip's parents, Petar and Nana Princip, lived a hard life in a house that had belonged to the Princip family for generations. This windowless dwelling was built from slabs of wood, with a steeply pitched roof. The doors were small and low, and the only light came through a hole in the roof which let out smoke from the open hearth. The family inhabited one large room. Their furniture consisted of a low table, wooden chests, cooking utensils, barrels of water, and chairs. At night the fire gave off a flickering light. Their dinners must have resembled the gloomy scene depicted in Van Gogh's painting, *The Potato Eaters*. A small, separate room contained a bed.

Unlike Gavrilo Princip, Franz Ferdinand had his choice of many rooms. The Archduke lived in Konopischt Castle in Bohemia thirty miles south of Prague. The castle had eighty-two rooms and was filled with light from high, leaded-glass windows. Outside were acres of carefully groomed laurels, hedges, and flower gardens. Franz Ferdinand acquired Konopischt Castle in 1887 when he was a bachelor of twenty-four and intent on restoring the castle's earlier glory. The Archduke was an avid collector of antiques and art, and he filled his newly acquired castle with these treasures. In addition, he personally supervised the cultivation of the gardens—featuring roses—on about forty acres of surrounding land.

But this was not all. At Konopischt, Franz Ferdinand hosted elaborate hunts. He and his guests killed stags and other game in the thousands. He was a doting father and treated his children to trips to Belvedere, the Habsburg castle in Vienna. There he and Sophie hosted elaborate receptions and balls, and the children were allowed to stay up and watch through the enormous windows of the castle as the glittering array of guests arrived in splendid carriages. During summer, the family spent time in the mountains at Chlumetz and at Bluhnbach near Salzburg, where the Archduke had acquired more property for his hunting. After Christmas, they traveled for several weeks to Switzerland and in the early spring to a spa on the Adriatic.

Meanwhile, times were hard for the Princip family. Nana Princip gave birth to nine children, six of whom died in infancy. Petar Princip worked about four acres of land and was required to pay one-third of the value of all his produce to his Muslim landlord. He could not grow enough grain to feed his family so, to supplement his income, Petar drove his wagon over the mountains from Bosnia to Dalmatia, carrying mail and passengers for a few coins.

Gavrilo Princip was a sickly, undersized baby—yet he did not die. Quiet and withdrawn, he preferred to watch peasants working the fields than to play with other children. At age nine, he attended a primary school two miles away from home and soon became an avid student and reader.

In childhood and early adolescence, Princip was brought up with tales of the Serbian past that chronicled the Serbian struggle for independence. He grew up hoping that one day his people would be freed from their Muslim overlords and Austrian administrators, and to be united in a Greater

Serbia. In the countryside where Princip lived, Bosnian Serbs gathered in the evenings around open fires where they drank plum brandy from earthenware cups and complained about the Austrian decision to occupy and later annex the Serbian lands of Bosnia and Hercegovina. These illiterate peasants kept alive the spark of Serbian nationalism by singing *guslas*, songs that invoked three themes: Serbian heroes, hatred of the Turks, and hatred of the Austrians. These scenes made a lasting impression on Princip. As he later wrote, "The wet logs on the open fire gave the only light to the closely packed peasants and their wives, wrapped in thick smoke. If I tried to penetrate the curtain of smoke, the most I could see were the eyes of the human beings, numerous, sad, and glaring with some kind of fluid light coming from nowhere. Some kind of reproach, even threat, radiated from them, and many times since they have awakened me from my dreams."

In 1907, the thirteen-year-old Princip came to Sarajevo to enroll in school. From his home, it was a three-day ride through the mountains to get to the nearest railroad station. Then it was an hour train ride to reach Sarajevo. At the time, Princip was a slight youth, dark-haired and dark-eyed with high cheekbones and a small, pouting mouth. His older brother, Jovo, paid Gavrilo's tuition from money he had earned with his team hauling logs from the forests to the mills.

Because the Austrians forbade schoolboys and other students to form organizations or associations, Princip and his fellow Serb students met in secret to discuss literature, ethics, and politics. In June 1910, a young Hercegovinian Serb named Zerajic attempted to assassinate the Austrian appointed governor of Sarajevo, failed, and then shot himself in the head. Zerajic's "act of courage" captured the imagination of the nationalist students of Bosnia and Hercegovina. Princip, who was barely sixteen, revered Zerajic. He vowed to someday attempt a similar assassination.

Many of Princip's compatriots believed that the purest element of the Serb race was in Bosnia and Hercegovina and that it was the duty of every young man in these territories to strive for a union with Serbia—in other words, to find the will and means to achieve a Greater Serbia. The Serbian Orthodox Church supported the concept and identified itself with "the Serbian soul." The largest newspaper in Sarajevo, *Srpska Rijec*, was vociferously pro-Serbian and found fault with everything the Austrian administration did. By 1907, articles were appearing in other newspapers in the region describing Austrians as "vampires and oppressors" and exclaiming that it was the duty of Serbs "to identify themselves with the fate of Serbia, their country and their brethren . . . If the call to arms rings out we have many reasons to respond to it, and to join those who are fighting to defend their freedom and their country . . . Our people have been deprived of national self-expression for thirty years."

In 1912, at age eighteen, Princip, having done poorly at school, dropped out against the wishes of his brother. He left Sarajevo and walked fifty difficult miles to Belgrade, the capital of Serbia. According to one account, when Princip crossed the frontier into Serbia, he fell on his knees and kissed the soil. In Belgrade, he found other disheveled and unemployed young men who worked as laborers during the day and, in the evenings, gathered in cheap cafes and coffee houses where, for the price of a single cup of coffee, they would sit for hours and talk about the iniquities of the region's major occupying power. Muslim landlords were bad, but the neighboring Austrians were worse.

While he was in the Serbian capitol, Princip volunteered for the *komitadjis*, an underground militia poised to advance into Macedonia under the command of Major Vojin Tankosic. The major, however, took one look at the pale, slightly stooped, undersized youth and told him he was unfit for any kind of military service. Humiliated by his rejection, Princip returned to Bosnia and lodged with his brother outside of Sarajevo. He retreated into reading, leading an inward life, still hoping to accomplish a deed that would advance the cause of his people.

During the following months, Princip moved back and forth between Belgrade and Sarajevo. While he was in Sarajevo in 1913, Austrian officials declared a state of emergency, enforced martial law, took control of the schools, and then banned all Serb associations. When Princip returned to Belgrade in February of 1914, he met Trifko Grabez, a Bosnian about his age, and renewed his acquaintance with Nedeljko Cabrinovic. These three young Bosnians looked for an opportunity to contribute to the liberation of their kinsmen.

In the spring of 1914, Princip read in a German newspaper that Archduke Franz Ferdinand and his wife would visit Bosnia for several days in June. Princip asked Grabez and Cabrinovic if they would join in a plot to assassinate the Archduke. They readily agreed. Princip wrote a letter to Danilo Ilic, a friend in Sarajevo who agreed to recruit other conspirators. The young assassins had no money to buy weapons, so in Belgrade they approached a Serbian guerrilla leader, or *komitadjis*, named Milan Ciganovic. Ciganovic was a twenty-six-year-old Bosnian Serb who held a minor position in the Serbian state railway. He had come to Belgrade in 1908 from Bosnia, volunteered for the *komitadjis*, served with them during the Balkan wars, and was well-known to their leader, Major Tankosic. Ciganovic told Tankosic of the plot. The major remembered Princip, the skinny volunteer. Could such an unlikely physical specimen possibly succeed? After nearly three weeks of deliberation, Tankosic told Ciganovic to teach the three youths how to fire a pistol.

In woods on the outskirts of Belgrade, Princip and his friends practiced firing at trees. Forty-eight hours later, Ciganovic produced the assassination weapons. They consisted of four Browning pistols each loaded with seven rounds, four loaded with reserve magazines, and six bombs filled with nails and pieces of lead. Each pistol was a 7.65 mm caliber, a Browning 1900 that had been manufactured at the Fabrique Nationale plant in Liege, Belgium. Here was a pistol with an indisputable American design—Utah's John M. Browning was its author. The pistols were probably shipped from Belgium to Belgrade to assist the Serbs in their 1912 war with Turkey. Each bomb was the size of a large cake of soap, was fitted with a safety cap, and weighed about two pounds. Ciganovic showed Princip and his two friends how to detonate the bombs. First, unscrew the safety cap. Second, knock the bomb against something hard. Third, throw it at the target—it would then explode in 10 to 13 seconds. He also provided the young men with packets of cyanide to take after the assassination so that an interrogation would not reveal the source of the plot.

Did Major Tankosic share the plan to assassinate the Archduke with higher Serbian officials? Very likely Tankosic contacted the leader of the Black Hand, a Serbian nationalist guerrilla group, led by thirty-four-year-old Major Dragutin Dimitrijevic. The major was often referred to as Apis and was an intelligent, courageous, captivating, ruthless, and fanatical Serb patriot. The historian Lavender Cassels sketches the most likely encounter between Tankosic and Apis, "One day Tankosic . . . said that he was being pestered by some young Bosnians who wanted to return home, and asked whether they should be allowed to go. Apis said he authorized this without stopping to think. When Tankosic added that these youths, together with their associates in Bosnia, intended to attempt 'something' against Franz Ferdinand, his reaction was that the Archduke would be so closely guarded that they would have no chance of trying to assassinate him, let alone succeeding in doing so. They might just conceivably stage some sort of incident. If they did, so much the better, it would serve as a warning to His Imperial Highness and his entourage that the Serbs were not to be trifled with."

Princip, and his friends, encumbered with four Browning pistols and six bombs, made the arduous journey from Belgrade to Sarajevo. They started on the morning of Ascension Day, May 28. When they arrived in a small border town, they contacted a certain Captain Popovic and told him they wanted to secretly cross the Drina River into Bosnia, but the captain said to go by train to another small town forty miles south and gave them a note to the frontier *gendarme* that read, "Look after these men and take them across where you think best." Princip said that he and his friends were short of money and so Popovic made out a warrant stating that they were three customs officials entitled to a reduction in train fare. During the train trip, a dispute arose between Princip and Cabrinovic because Princip felt that Cabrinovic was being indiscreet in sending out six or seven postcards to friends in Sarajevo, some of which contained passages from Serbian nationalist poems. With that, Princip told him he'd have to cross the border himself and meet again outside of Sarajevo. As it turned out, Cabrinovic managed a relatively comfortable and error-free trip into Bosnia. For Princip and Grabez, the journey was a bit different.

These two young men spent the night of May 31 on an island in the middle of the Drina River. At first light, a Serb peasant guided them through the shallow waters to the Bosnian shore, through a swamp on the other side of the river, and set them along a path through what seemed an endless forest. To make matters worse, rain began to beat down on them. Lugging their heavy armaments, soaked to the skin, and with their pants torn by brambles, they at last reached a ruined hut where they took shelter for the night.

The next day they reached the dwelling of a peasant who had been told to look after them. After resting for the night, they stuffed their pistols and bombs in a bag and proceeded along a steep, slippery trail until they reached a town called Priboj where, fearing they would attract attention, they hid in a thicket. How could they enter this town, dressed in conspicuously shabby and dirty clothes? That evening they were saved by another friendly peasant, this one on horseback, who told Princip and Grabez to follow him and took their two heavy bags on his saddle. This strange procession wandered into town to a house belonging to a man called Mitar Kerovic who, following Serbian tradition, gave Princip and Grabez warm food and dry beds. The next morning they set out in a peasant's cart, hiding beneath piles of hay. At this point, a contact named Jovanovic was waiting for them in a small town called Tuzla. After washing in a stream, Princip and Grabez showed up on Jovanovic's doorstep. Here they collected themselves, purchased new clothes, and reconnected with Cabrinovic. Laden with bombs and pistols, these three young men caught the next train to Sarajevo.

When Princip, Grabez, and Cabrinovic arrived in the Bosnian capitol, they made contact with Ilich and his recruits. By June 24, all the conspirators were in Sarajevo, and Princip and Ilich poured over the official program for the Archduke's visit. Because the Austrian-appointed governor, Oskar Potiorek, wanted to orchestrate an enthusiastic reception for the heir to the throne, the details of Franz Ferdinand's visit—timed to the minute—were published in the newspapers. Princip and Ilich now knew that Franz Ferdinand would arrive in the city by train at 9:50 AM. He would proceed from the station by car, visit the Sarajevo Town Hall, ceremonially open and tour a new museum, and lunch with Governor Potiorek before leaving the city. Franz Ferdinand's time in Sarajevo would be brief, a little less than four hours. Princip and Ilich reasoned that their best shot at the Archduke was at the station, the town hall, or the museum. After discussion, they decided to position the assassins (by now there were a total of six) along a 350 yard stretch of the royal motor route from the train station to the town hall.

Franz Ferdinand's journey to Sarajevo was far less arduous than that of Princip. It began when Emperor Wilhelm II visited Konopischt Castle the third week of June. Franz Ferdinand and Wilhelm—one the heir to the throne of the Habsburg monarchy, the other the leader of the German empire—walked in the sunlight through the rose gardens. Franz Ferdinand was dressed in a casual, civilian suit and sported a straw boater hat, the picture of ease and contentment. Wilhelm told him that the Russian armies were not yet ready for war. He argued that now would be the time to take a firm stand in the Balkans.

On June 24, Franz Ferdinand traveled alone in a special train coach to Trieste on the Italian coast. (Sophie would join him later.) He then boarded the Austrian battleship, *Viribus Unitis,* and steamed to the mouth of the Narenta River in southern Dalmatia. Next, he took a train to Ilidze in Bosnia where Sophie met him, having come earlier from Vienna by train. For all practical purposes, Ilidze was Franz Ferdinand's home base for his Bosnian visit. He and Sophie stayed at the Hotel Bosnia, an elaborate spa with balconies and carved woodwork. Their room was furnished with carved tables inlaid with mother of pearl, Oriental carpets, and *objects d'art* loaned by art dealers from nearby Sarajevo. Franz Ferdinand's primary official duty was to attend military maneuvers in mountainous terrain about fourteen miles west of Ilidze.

On the afternoon of Saturday, June 27, Princip and Ilich distributed the

(The Archduke Franz Ferdinand.)

bombs, Browning pistols, and packets of cyanide to the remaining assassins, instructing each that he was to take the cyanide after the killing. That evening, Princip joined some acquaintances in a tavern, where he seemed morose and sullen. He drained a glass of wine at a single gulp and then came alive with conversation. Later, he was reluctant to go back to his lodgings. It was as if he wanted to make the night last.

June 28, 1914 was a cloudless Sunday in Sarajevo and, by 9:00 AM, the temperature was already in the eighties. The train from Illidze pulled into the station a few minutes behind schedule, and a puffy-faced Franz Ferdinand and his wife stepped onto the platform. The Archduke was resplendent in the full-dress uniform of a cavalry general—a pale-blue tunic with a gold-braided collar and cuffs, a sash with a large, gilt tassel, black trousers with a double red stripe, and a hat adorned with green plumes. Sophie wore a feathered hat and a white silk dress with a red sash and carried a parasol. Franz Ferdinand was sweaty, impatient, and oblivious to a Sarajevo dotted with armed Serbian assassins who were bent on sending him into the next world.

The Archduke and his wife stepped into the backseat of an open car, the famous six-seater Double Phaeton which belonged to Count Franz Harrach. The royal procession began to slowly motor toward the town hall. Along the way, Princip and his fellow assassins waited dutifully at their positions along the Appel Quay. One of the spectators waiting to see the Archduke looked across the quay and saw a young man on the far pavement, standing curiously in the blazing sun. He was, noted the observer, "rather strangely dressed. He wore a black jacket which resembled a dinner jacket and dove grey trousers . . . The jacket was buttoned up, and as the youth looked in my direction I saw that he had thrust his right hand inside it, as though he wanted to hold on to something in his left inner breast pocket." The youth was Princip's friend, Cabrinovic—under his coat he was clutching one of the bombs.

In a few minutes, the procession came into Cabrinovic's sight, traveling no more than ten or twelve miles-an-hour, and each car twenty yards apart. As the Archduke's car passed, the first assassin lost his nerve and remained frozen. The second assassin in line also had a clear shot but did nothing. "When I saw the Archduke I could not bring myself to kill him," he said later. But Cabrinovic pulled the bomb from his pocket, unscrewed the safety cap, banged the bomb against the tramway mast to start the fuse, and heaved it straight at Franz Ferdinand.

The driver of the car heard the crack of the fuse—it sounded like a pistol shot—and instinctively accelerated. The bomb, therefore, landed on the folded canvas top behind the backseat of the Phaeton, fell to the pavement, and exploded. Cabrinovic tried to swallow his cyanide, but in his agitation spilled most of it. He ran, and so did four of the other assassins.

Franz Ferdinand ordered his car to halt. The car behind his bore the brunt of the explosion. One of its occupants, Potiorek's adjutant, was bleeding from a wound to his head, and several pedestrians had also been injured. Cabrinovic was quickly caught by police. Princip, farther along the dusty street, heard the explosion and assumed that Franz Ferdinand was dead. When the Archduke saw that no one had been killed and that the injured were being assisted, he ordered his car to proceed and soon passed by a surprised Princip as well as the last assassin, Princip's friend Grabez, who was stuck in the middle of the crowd.

The Phaeton arrived safely at the Sarajevo Town Hall, where Franz Ferdinand, wiping debris from his uniform, told the assembled Sarajevo officials, "So, I come here on a state visit and I get bombs thrown at me!"

This was not a happy group. The mayor and other city dignitaries were assembled in front of the town hall that had been built by the Austrians at the turn of the century in an imitation Turkish architecture with crudely fretted arches. Against this backdrop, Franz Ferdinand allowed the mayor, a Muslim, to proceed with his speech.

"Your imperial and royal Highness, our hearts are transported with happiness by your gracious visit," began the mayor. When he was finished with his speech, the Archduke delivered his prepared response, altering it at the end by declaring that the people's joy "over the failure of the attack" was but another proof of their loyalty and devotion to the crown.

Once inside the town hall, after more ceremony, the Archduke decided it would be appropriate to visit victims of the bombing in the hospital. Before departing, he needled Governor Potiorek about the sloppy security arrangements for his visit. Naturally, Potiorek took offense. "What," he said to the Archduke, "do you think that the streets of Sarajevo are filled with assassins?"

Franz Ferdinand looked at him with skeptical silence.

"I assure you, Your Excellency," Potiorek said, "that the rest of your visit will be quite uneventful."

With that the imperial couple left town hall and walked down the steps towards their waiting car. They had perhaps seven or eight minutes to live. As they stepped into the Phaeton, the local Bosnian dignitaries who lined the steps saluted, their gloved hands raised to their flower-pot hats, as if officiating at a funeral.

The procession continued through the streets of Sarajevo. Princip's friend, Grabez, saw the cars coming but did nothing. The procession passed by him. And then, in one of those strange twists of fate, after passing Grabez, the Archduke's driver took a wrong turn, realized his mistake, and brought the Phaeton to a halt before backing up.

At this moment, Princip was sitting at a sidewalk table outside of Schiller's delicatessen shop just a few feet from the motionless car that carried Franz Ferdinand and his wife. Understandably surprised once again, Princip rose, holding the Browning pistol in his pocket. He walked a few paces until even with the royal couple in the backseat of the Phaeton, pulled out his Browning, and fired twice. The first shot tore through the car door, striking Sophie. The second shot penetrated Franz Ferdinand's neck. Just after the shots were fired, Sophie turned to her husband. A thin stream of blood began to trickle from the Archduke's mouth. "In God's name, what has happened to you?" she said. Then Sophie collapsed, her head between her husband's knees. Most witnesses assumed she had fainted. "Sophie! Sophie!" Franz Ferdinand said, "Don't die! Live for my children."

(Later, when Princip was on trial and a lawyer asked him if he was moved by these final words, Princip replied, "Do you think I am an animal?") As officials rushed to his aid, the Archduke was heard to repeat, "*Es ist nichts. Es ist nichts.*" (It is nothing. It is nothing.) Both husband and wife died a few minutes later.

At the trial, all the accused pleaded guilty except Princip, who said, "I am not a criminal because I have killed a man who has done wrong; I think I have done right." Aside from killing Sophie, he had no regrets. When the old Emperor Franz Josef heard the news about his nephew, he paused and closed his eyes. "A higher power," he said, "has restored that order which unfortunately I was unable to maintain."

III

INDEED, FRANZ JOSEF HAD NEVER LIKED FRANZ FERDINAND. Their disagreement over the Archduke's choice of a wife was only the first of many. Yet their disagreements were for the most part a private matter. Nearly all the Austrian principals viewed the assassination as a pretext to act against Serbia. And Edward Grey later reflected, "No crime has ever aroused deeper or more general horror throughout Europe . . . Sympathy for Austria was universal. Both government and public opinion were ready to support her in any measures, however severe, which she might think it necessary to take for the punishment of the murderer and his accomplices."

Edward Grey had no way of knowing that a mere thirty-seven days separated the killing of Franz Ferdinand from the outbreak of World War One.

Day One. London. June 29.

British Foreign Secretary Grey sent a telegram to his Austrian counterpart, Count Mensdorff, and expressed his concern about the effect of the assassination on Emperor Franz Josef—the grand old figurehead who had always been vigilant about maintaining the European peace. Grey paced the rooms of the Foreign Office along Whitehall in London. It was a beautiful summer and the rooms of his office were uncomfortably warm. He sought to fashion a diplomatic solution to the assassination of Franz Ferdinand—the latest of many disputes on the continent. Surely Grey thought such trouble in the Balkans could be cast in the light of a purely local affair, a local argument or family problem that would end with some shouting back and forth and a double funeral."

Grey's concept of Sarajevo as a local incident resonated with the five London diplomats who were determined to prevent a general war at all costs. Each was his country's respective ambassador to Britain. Lichnowsky of Germany, Mensdorff of Austria, Imperial of Italy, Cambon of France, and Benckendorff of Russia—along with Grey himself—composed a group one might describe as the London Six. They were men of intelligence, foresight, and good intentions. They had worked together for nearly a decade. They were friends. Surely their civility, good judgment, and sense of proportion would win the day.

Grey and his colleagues were confident that they could peacefully resolve this "foolish" thing which had happened in the Balkans. It was a matter of how one *viewed* the problem, the importance one attached to it, the ability to weigh it carefully and give it perspective.

There had been no significant loss of life in Europe since 1870. These were years of peace, and this brave, sunlit summer was one of the most peaceful of all. As Grey paced his rooms, families all over Europe were taking long walks in the country. 1914 was a summer of wine and parties and children splashing in sun-dappled rivers. Men and women ate bread and cheese in outdoor cafes, or made love in their summer apartments, throwing open the windows to the warm night air. Europeans lived with the expectation that September and October would fall into place as calmly as had June and July.

The summer of 1914 was a time when it appeared to the public that peace could be arranged as easily as an international wedding or a contract between two prominent companies from separate countries. Europeans had grown used to peace. War—particularly a general war—would be a jarring, unexpected failure. Each of the London Six—Lichnowsky, Mensdorff, Imperial, Cambon, Benckendorff, and Grey—were decent, civilized men, the product of the finest schools and most advanced training. They were the cream of their respective societies, the fond hope of their people for the future. None of their nations were ruled by men who seemed to favor war. Certainly the German Kaiser and Franz Josef of Austria appeared receptive to a reasonable, negotiated solution. There was no reason that the London Six need fail. If the situation became grave, Grey reasoned, he and his colleagues could always convene a six power conference.

Unfortunately, the London Six were battling against unseen opponents, three men in Berlin and Vienna who could be called the Dark Troika. They included the German chancellor, Theobald von Bethmann-Hollweg, the German foreign minister, Gottlieb von Jagow, and the Austrian foreign minister, Count Leopold Berchtold. Of the three, Bethmann-Hollweg was in the best position to arrest or to orchestrate war. A tall, broad-shouldered man of fifty-two with a silver Vandyke beard, Bethmann-Hollweg was determined to engineer with his two co-conspirators what he thought would be a localized war against Serbia. All three kept their counterparts in London in the dark. Moreover, Franz Josef, the ruler of Austria, and to some extent Kaiser Wilhelm of Germany, became unwitting dupes to the scheme.

The diplomatic maneuvering that July was an elaborate and deadly chess game that faced off the London Six against the Dark Troika, a trio bent on war. Grey and his fellow diplomats appeared to have everything going for them, yet they actually were at a disadvantage. They had no idea who their real opponents were.

Day Four. Vienna. July 2.

Emperor Franz Josef consulted his aides during a state meeting held in his office late in the morning. After deliberating, he finally agreed to draft a note to the Kaiser, seeking the assurance and support of his ally should Austria invade Serbia in retaliation for Franz Ferdinand's murder. That afternoon Franz Josef reflected upon the death of his nephew.

For the Emperor, the assassination was the most recent in a long series of events that had established his reign as a political and personal disaster. At the time of the assassination, Franz Josef was eighty-four years old. He had ruled for sixty-six years. From the beginning, very little had gone right. During the first years, he lost the northern Italian provinces of Lombardy and Venice. In 1866, he lost a significant battle to the Prussians. The following year his brother, Maximilian, who had been installed as emperor of Mexico, was brought up on charges and shot by a Mexican firing squad. In addition, Franz Josef's only son killed himself and his mistress in a suicide pact. The Emperor was unlucky in marriage, too. After only six years of wedlock, his beautiful wife, Elisabeth, bolted from his bedside to wander across Europe. He always hoped she would return. When, forty years later, she was murdered by an anarchist, Franz Josef said, "Nothing has been spared me in this world." In the summer of 1914, the challenge to his authority from a group of impoverished, renegade Slavs made the Emperor determined to maintain whatever power the Austro-Hungarian Empire still possessed.

DAY SEVEN. BERLIN. JULY 5.

A week after the assassination, the Austrian ambassador to Germany, Count Szogyeny, joined Kaiser Wilhelm for lunch to deliver the note Franz Josef had composed three days earlier. "The crime against my nephew," read the Emperor's note, "is the directed consequence of agitation carried on by Russian and Serbian Pan-Slavists whose sole aim is to weaken the Triple Alliance and shatter my Empire. The bloody deed was not the work of a single individual but a well-organized plot whose threads extend to Belgrade . . . What would German policy be if Austria decided to punish this center of criminal agitation in Belgrade?"

The Kaiser read through the letter, then raised his eyes to Count Szogyeny, and said that the situation was complex, and that he would have to speak with his chancellor before formulating a response. After lunch, however, he used less caution. At this point the Kaiser, not his chancellor and the other two members of the Dark Troika, appeared to lead the rush to war.

Kaiser Wilhelm told his guest that Austria could "count on Germany's full support" and he underscored how propitious this moment was for a strike at Serbia. Time could not be wasted. No doubt Russia would be hostile. And yet, he explained, "Russia is in no way prepared for war." Later that day, German Chancellor Bethmann-Hollweg endorsed the Kaiser's blank check. "The views of the Kaiser corresponded with my own," he later noted in his memoirs.

Wilhelm's post-lunch comments forged the next link in the chain of events. Had he acted with caution, Edward Grey might have had the time to assemble the Six-Power summit he envisioned. But caution and prudence were not part of the Kaiser's makeup. He was brash and impetuous. He also equivocated and frequently changed his mind. In the days to come, would he step back from his reckless after-lunch statements?

Perhaps the imperfections in the Kaiser's personality can be attributed to regrets about his country and his own person. Born with a shrunken and enfeebled left arm, Wilhelm was forced to have his meat cut for him. He was the grandson of Queen Victoria, and his lengthy visits to the English royal retreat on the Isle of Wight fostered his desire for a German navy.

"When, as a little boy, I was allowed to visit Portsmouth and Plymouth hand in hand with kind aunts and friendly admirals. I admired the proud English ships in those two superb harbors. Then there awoke in me the wish to build ships of my own like these someday, and when I was grown up to possess as fine a navy as the English." After Bismarck's death, in a challenge to British command of the seas, the Kaiser embarked upon an aggressive campaign to build ships of his own. Although the German navy played only a small role in World War One, it was nevertheless the presence of the navy that gave the Kaiser confidence to launch the war, even at the risk of provoking Britain.

Kaiser Wilhelm II was an active monarch. His energy and ambition were evident early on. He had lectured German troops departing for China in 1905 to fight in the Boxer Rebellion and asked them to conduct themselves with the same ferocity as the Huns of Attila. (Note how the label "Hun" managed to stick to German troops during both world wars.) Throughout his reign, and particularly in the summer of 1914, the Kaiser continued to rant about the slights to his country, about the perfidy of his enemies, about *Einkreisung* (encirclement). In November 1913, he invited King Albert I of Belgium for a state dinner.

At a court ball prior to the dinner, the Kaiser, walking beside the young king, pointed out a fierce-looking German general, Alexander von Kluck. "You see that man. He will be leading the march upon Paris." Though obsessed with destroying France, the Kaiser was even more preoccupied with the Russians. His first cousin, Czar Nicholas II, was, in the Kaiser's view, "only fit to live in a country house and grow turnips." Nevertheless, Wilhelm continued to blitz the poor man with letters and telegrams—"My advice to you is more speeches and more parades . . ."—partly because he wanted Nicholas under his thumb and partly because he wanted to woo him away from Russia's treaty obligations with France. "I hate the Slavs," he once confessed to an Austrian officer. "I know it is a sin to do so. We ought not to hate anyone. But I can't help hating them."

DAY EIGHT. LONDON. JULY 6.

Grey and the German ambassador, Lichnowsky, spoke privately and confidentially during the afternoon in Grey's office. The Austrians, Lichnowsky warned, intended to take action against Serbia—such action might mean the use of force. But no Serbian territory would be seized, he assured Grey. This would just be a minor action—a local affair between two neighbors—nothing more.

Prince Karl Max Lichnowsky was Grey's closest colleague among the London Six. He was a distinguished, silver-haired gentleman who prided himself on the Anglo portion of his Anglo-Germanic heritage. According to one historian, Lichnowsky "had come to London determined to make himself and his country liked." He "spoke English and copied English manners, sports, and dress in a strenuous endeavor to become the very pattern of an English gentleman . . . To the ambassador no tragedy could be greater than war between the country of his birth and the country of his heart."

Lichnowsky explained to Grey that Germany was placed in a difficult situation. If Germany held Austria back, she would be accused of neglecting her ally at a critical moment. If Germany allowed Austria to have a free hand at retaliating against Serbia, the chance of a larger war would grow.

Part of Grey's concern stemmed from his inability to deal directly with Austria. The dual alliance between Austria and Germany severely limited the scope of any Anglo-Austrian rapprochement. During the previous three or four years, Grey had faced a puzzle: was Berlin pushing Vienna? Or, on the other hand, was Vienna pushing Berlin?

Lichnowsky told Grey to use his influence at St. Petersburg, since Germany was apprehensive about what Russia might do if Austria laid too heavy a hand on Serbia. In one respect, Lichnowsky's concerns about Russia comforted Grey. They confirmed that members of the "German government are in a peaceful mood and that they are very anxious to be on good terms with England."

DAY TEN. LONDON. JULY 8.

Grey received the Russian ambassador, Count Benckendorff, in his office and warned him that Austria might seek severe reprisal measures against Serbia. If so, Russian restraint would be appropriate.

Count Benckendorff, along with Grey and the German Lichnowsky, formed the inner circle of the London Six. In many respects, these three men held the fate of Europe in their hands.

On this morning, Benckendorff and Grey discussed the issue of Austrian reprisals for nearly half-an-hour. Count Benckendorff told Grey that he hoped Germany would keep Austria in check. Whatever the Germans might feel, there was no ill-will in St. Petersburg. Grey urged the Russians to do all they could to convince Germany that no coup or military action was being prepared against her.

DAY ELEVEN. LONDON. JULY 9.

As the first order of business, Grey sent a messenger to the German Embassy to request that Lichnowsky join him in person at the Foreign Office.

When Lichnowsky arrived, Grey reassured him that there were no secret agreements between Great Britain and France or Russia. Lichnowsky urged that Grey use his influence with Britain's other *entente* partners, particularly France. Grey responded that, "England wished to preserve an absolutely free hand so that in the event of Continental complications she might be able to act according to her judgment." Grey referred to the various naval or military conversations conducted between Britain and France since 1906, but said that they did not constitute agreements and therefore brought no obligations. Britain would have a free hand in helping diffuse this crisis. Grey told Lichnowsky that he hoped Austria—and particularly Franz Josef—would see that strong reprisals against Serbia might lead to a larger war. Britain "had been endeavoring to persuade the Russian Government even at the present juncture to adopt a calm view and a conciliatory attitude toward Austria, should the Vienna Cabinet feel obliged in consequence of the Sarajevo murder to take up a stern attitude toward Serbia."

Grey pressed Lichnowsky. It was critical, he told the German ambassador, that Austria not provoke Russia by arousing Slav feeling. Both men were peacemakers and, at that time, both believed this tempest would pass. In fact, that same day, Grey's principal diplomatic advisor, Sir Arthur Nicolson, wrote, "I have my doubts as to whether Austria will take any action of a serious character and I expect the storm will blow over."

DAY SIXTEEN. LONDON. JULY 14.

Prince Lichnowsky wrote a letter to the leader of the Dark Troika, German Chancellor Bethmann. In his letter, Lichnowsky commented that the Austrians had only themselves to blame for sending the heir to their throne into a seething pot of Serb assassins, "an alley of bomb throwers" as he described it. Lichnowsky counseled restraint—and perhaps with Grey's concerns in mind—warned that nobody wanted to aggravate the Russians. Storm clouds were gathering and Lichnowsky recognized them.

DAY EIGHTEEN. LONDON. JULY 16.

As Grey waited for Austria's response to Serbia, his anxieties over Germany increased. He suspected that Lichnowsky had not accurately conveyed the German government's attitude on Austrian matters. The Austrian ultimatum to Serbia went through a series of drafts. Unknown to Edward Grey in London, the Austrians sent each draft to the German government. Germany approved the wording and the wording was harsh. As one Austrian diplomat put it, "The note is being composed so that the possibility of its acceptance is practically excluded."

For the time being, Grey was willing to suspend judgment on Germany, willing to give Ambassador Lichnowsky's good will more time. Yet both men were in the dark and had no understanding that their passivity at this moment was allowing the last grains of peace to slip from their fingers.

As one historian put it, "To avoid alarming the rest of Europe and to create the impression that Berlin, like other capitals, was wondering how Vienna would respond to Sarajevo, the Wilhelmstrasse deliberately and repeatedly lied to foreign diplomats of other governments. The three villains—Bethmann-Hollweg, Berchtold, and Jagow—were hard at work. When the British, French, and Russian ambassadors called at the Foreign Office to ask what Germany knew of her ally's intentions, the Wilhelmstrasse soothingly declared that it regarded the situation with tranquility; were not the Kaiser, the Chancellor, and all the military chiefs on vacation?"

DAY TWENTY-THREE. ST. PETERSBURG. JULY 21.

Russian Foreign Minister Sazonov told Count Pourtales, the German ambassador in St. Petersburg, that Russia would do its best to persuade Belgrade to make reasonable amends, but he warned that the Austrian note must not be an ultimatum. As the Austrian list of demands reached its final draft, both the Austrian and German governments assumed that Russia would not intervene in a localized war between Austria and Serbia. Yet the Russians had never told either government that they would remain passive.

Unfortunately, the note *was* an ultimatum. And the Austrians had worded it to avoid compromise. The timing of the ultimatum's delivery was critical, and Count Berchtold, the Austrian member of the Dark Troika, made certain that the ultimatum was delivered at a time when it would most certainly lead to war on terms most favorable to Austria and Germany.

Originally, the date for delivery to Belgrade had been set for July 18, but Berchtold remembered that French President Raymond Poincare would be making a state visit to St. Petersburg at the time. "We should consider it unwise to undertake the threatening step in Belgrade at the very time when the peace-loving, reserved Czar Nicholas and the undeniably cautious Herr Sazonov are under the influence of the two who are always for war, Isvolvsky (the Russian Ambassador in Paris), and Poincare."

DAY TWENTY-FIVE. ST. PETERSBURG. JULY 23.

French President Poincare and French Foreign Minister Rene Viviani left the Russian capital aboard the battleship *France*.

DAY TWENTY-FIVE. BELGRADE. JULY 23.

Baron Vladimir von Giesl, the Austrian minister at Belgrade, delivered the Austro-Hungarian ultimatum to the acting Serbian prime minister, Finance Minister Pacu. The time was 6:00 PM. The Serbs had forty-eight hours to respond, although none of the leaders were quite prepared for the draconian contents of the ultimatum. It listed ten demands, including the closure of all Serbian publications critical of Austria-Hungary, the recall of all schoolbooks that took positions against Austria, and the arrest of certain officials and officers named in the ultimatum. The document also demanded that Austrian officials be allowed to monitor the changes inside Serbia. These were extreme demands—much like those that a victorious state would impose upon a defeated one. Of course, Serbia and Austria were not yet at war, although the rigid and pernicious demands were designed to provoke war rather than to ensure peace.

Because the ultimatum had a time limit of forty-eight hours, its acceptance or rejection would occur on July 25, while French President Poincare was still at sea.

DAY TWENTY-SIX. LONDON. JULY 24.

At 2:00 PM, the Austrian ambassador in London, Count Mensdorff, handed a copy of the ultimatum to Grey at the Foreign Office. Grey characterized the note as "the most formidable document ever addressed from one state to another." All at once, Grey realized, Bismarck's prediction that "some damn foolish thing in the Balkans will cause the next big war" was coming true.

In the afternoon, Grey brought up the Serbian crisis toward the end of the Cabinet meeting. Until this time, the foreign secretary had consulted only Asquith, Haldane, and Winston Churchill. (He had no wish to involve the pacifist wing of the Cabinet.)

Churchill recalled the moment. "The discussion had reached its inconclusive end, and the Cabinet was about to separate, when the quiet grave tones of Sir Edward Grey's voice were heard reading a document which had just been brought to him from the Foreign Office. It was the Austrian note to Serbia. He had been reading or speaking for several minutes before I could disengage my mind from the tedious and bewildering debate which had just closed . . . This note was clearly an ultimatum; but it was an ultimatum such as had never been penned in modern times . . . The parishes of Fermanagh and Tyrone faded back into the mists and squalls of Ireland, and a strange light began immediately, but by perceptible gradations, to fall and grow upon the map of Europe."

Grey expressed his deepest concerns. The Austrians, it seemed, were playing with matches, and whether or not Russia would come to the aid of Serbia seemed of little consequence to them. The note had been drafted so that it could not, as a whole, be accepted. The Austro-Hungarian ultimatum could be the prelude to a war in which at least four of the leading European powers would be involved.

Day Twenty-seven. London. July 25.

At mid-morning, Lichnowsky arrived at Grey's office and read him a telegram from the Wilhelmstrasse confirming that Germany had no previous knowledge of the text of the Austrian ultimatum.

The truth, of course, was that the Dark Troika in Berlin and Vienna had concealed their developing war plans from Lichnowsky.

On this morning, Lichnowsky was eager to hear Grey's peace proposals. Because of the severity of the Austrian demand, Grey told Lichnowsky that his chances of restraining Russia were now more difficult. In fact, the pressure was now in the other direction.

Day Twenty-seven. London. July 25.

Late in the morning, Grey received a telegram from Moscow in which Sazonov told him he expected Britain to honor her agreements with Russia. With Sazonov's message, the chance of holding in check the upcoming war was nearly gone.

France had already joined the Russians in the war camp. Two days earlier, Poincare and Viviani had concluded talks in the Russian capital where they supported the firm line taken by Russia. Therefore, Sazonov's appeal to Grey was delivered with the hope that England should not try to enlist French support in holding back Russia. Whatever Grey thought of the Austrian case, France and Russia had decided to make a stand.

Grey was now faced with a decision. Should he put the British fleet on a war footing, as Churchill urged him to do? Still, the time was too early to make decisions that he could not retract. Even though he knew that events were spiraling toward war, Grey still held out hope. He did not want to adopt any policy that would firmly and irretrievably align Britain with one side or the other. That afternoon, at the height of the crisis, Edward Grey left London to visit his fishing cottage on the River Itchen.

The difficulties facing Grey on this day were enormous. Still, unlike George Custer and Thomas Andrews, Edward Grey was, for the most part, in control of his plan. Custer lost control when he split his forces and gave orders to attack the Indian village on the Little Bighorn River. Andrews never had control of his ship after its design, and, as the *Titanic* listed in the North Atlantic, he would see how faulty human judgment and failures of technology doomed his ship.

When Edward Grey departed London for his cottage, the choices he faced were daunting. If he sided with Russia and France and allowed Churchill to put the navy on a war footing, he might deter the Germans and the Austrians. It might then be possible to mediate the Austrian-Serbian conflict. If he succeeded, Grey would silence the naysayers. Yet, he would then find himself forced to align Britain closer to Germany to make up for what would be an egregious diplomatic defeat for Berlin. On the other hand, such a bold policy stood little chance of being adopted given the mistrust of the British public toward Germany. Another obstacle to British-German rapprochement: this Serbian issue seemed too small for a complete reversal of Grey's policy of the balance of powers.

Day Twenty-seven. Belgrade. July 25.

5:00 PM. Pasic, the Serbian president, walked to the Austrian embassy and delivered his country's response to the Austrian ultimatum. The response was delivered one hour before the forty-eight hour deadline stipulated by the Austrians was to pass. The Serbian answer had evolved into a massive document, for the Serbian Cabinet had kept amending it. The only available typewriter had jammed so the Serbs had resorted to handwriting. Pasic handed this envelope to Baron Giesl, the formal Austrian waiting at the embassy, and said in broken German, "Part of your demands we have accepted, for the rest we place our hopes on your loyalty and chivalry as an Austrian general."

The Serbian government accepted all the Austrian demands except one: the demand that Austrian officers be allowed to participate in the judicial inquiry into the plot that had resulted in the Archduke's assassination. This, the Serbs claimed, would be a violation of their constitution and their laws of criminal procedure. Unfortunately, the recipient of this note, Baron Giesl, glanced down at its contents, noted the single sticking point, and according to instructions from his superior, grabbed his already-packed bags and departed the country.

Day Twenty-eight. London. July 26.

Grey returned to London from his cottage on an afternoon train. He did not know of the Serbian reply or the Austrian refusal to accept it.

Grey had decided to head off war by reconvening a six power conference—the same conference which had mediated Balkan problems in the past. At that moment, the same ambassadors who had attended earlier six power conferences were still in London.

Under orders from Grey, Sir Arthur Nicolson, Grey's diplomatic advisor, sent a draft of Grey's peace conference proposal to foreign ministers in Paris, Rome, and Berlin. Lichnowsky followed by firing off a barrage of telegrams to Germany's foreign minister, Herr Gottlieb von Jagow. But Jagow was a stalwart of the Dark Troika. He was no more interested in peace than the even worse Austrian villain, Foreign Minister Berchtold.

"If our respective governments would only use us and trust us and give us the chance," Grey wrote, "we could keep the peace of Europe . . . an honorable peace, no vaunting [boasting] on one side and humiliation on another."

Grey realized that the one country that could solve this crisis was Germany. In a sense, Germany was Austria's parent—authority for a fight would have to come from her. Both Grey and Lichnowsky strenuously desired peace. In Berlin, Kaiser Wilhelm's impetuous warlike statements normally would soon be followed by equally impetuous statements that thrust in the opposite direction and effectively corrected his policy. In this case, however, the Kaiser's staff made certain that he did not retreat from his ill-considered, warlike remarks until it was too late.

The Kaiser was off on a three-week-long sailing trip in Norwegian waters. He communicated via telegram while he was gone, so he was able to follow developments. But this form of communication made it easy for the German chancellor and his colleagues in Berlin and Vienna to conceal their war plans. Had the Kaiser been in Berlin, had he examined Chancellor Bethmann face-to-face, he undoubtedly would have quickly corrected his earlier hard-line position. For his part, Lichnowsky was not in a position to prod the Kaiser to inject probity and reason into the situation, because Lichnowsky had no idea that war plans were rushing forward.

The language of the dispatches from Lichnowsky to Jagow betrays a sense of urgency that was obviously shared by Grey.

> Sir E. Grey had me call on him just now . . . [He had just read] the Serbian reply to the Austrian note. It appeared to him that Serbia had agreed to the Austrian demands to an extent such as he would have never believed possible . . . Should Austria fail to be satisfied with this reply . . . it would then be absolutely evident that Austria was only seeking an excuse for crushing Serbia . . . I found the Minister [Grey] irritated for the first time. He spoke with great seriousness and seemed absolutely to expect that we should successfully make use of our influence to settle the matter . . . Everybody here is convinced that the key to the situation is to be found in Berlin and that if peace is seriously desired there, Austria can be restrained from prosecuting—as Sir E. Grey expressed it—a foolhardy policy.

DAY TWENTY-NINE. BERLIN. JULY 27.

Kaiser Wilhelm returned from his sailing trip. He arrived in Berlin late in the day. Chancellor Bethmann waited on the railway platform, overworked, exhausted, and pale. By now, the Kaiser had learned of the Austrian ultimatum, and he was aghast. In contradiction to his after-lunch remarks of July 5, the Kaiser expressed extreme dismay that his chancellor had brought the nation to the brink of war.

"How did it all happen?" he said irritably to an unsettled chancellor. Instead of responding directly, Bethmann offered to resign.

"No," said the Kaiser, "you've cooked this broth and now you're going to eat it."

DAY TWENTY-NINE. VIENNA. JULY 27.

The Austrian Foreign Minister Count Berchtold met Austrian Emperor Franz Josef in the evening to convince him to sign a declaration of war against Serbia. With an eerie echo of the beginning of World War Two (when Nazis faked a Polish attack against German border guards), Berchtold overcame the doubts of Franz Josef by sending him a telegram describing a completely fictitious Serbian attack on an Austro-Hungarian border detachment. Franz Josef signed the declaration.

DAY THIRTY. BERLIN. JULY 28.

Early in the morning, the Kaiser read the Serbian response to the Austrian ultimatum. He was pleased and told his ministers, "A brilliant performance for a time limit of only forty-eight hours. This is more than one could have expected. A great moral victory for Vienna; with it every reason for war drops away."

The Kaiser ordered Bethmann to initiate immediate mediation between Austria and Serbia. For Bethmann and Jagow this presented a problem. After all, the purpose of the ultimatum was to ensure rejection and provide the basis for war. What was one to do? Bethmann decided to do nothing. He simply ignored the Kaiser's request and told the German ambassador in Vienna that he must "avoid very carefully giving rise to the impression that we wish to hold Austria back."

The Dark Troika in Berlin and Vienna was in no mood to compromise. They had channeled events toward war. Austria's foreign minister, Berchtold, had convinced an irritable Franz Josef to call for limited Austrian mobilization. The Austrians were determined to punish the Serbs. The stage for such an event would be a localized war, small enough to keep Russia from getting involved.

July 27 and July 28 were critical days in the crisis. Unfortunately, the conspirators in Berlin and Vienna held most of the cards. The added ingredients of fraud, villainy, and deception by the Dark Troika played a decisive role in the hasty transactions of these two days.

Although Edward Grey did not know it on July 28, the catalyst for war lay in the hands of German Chancellor Bethmann and Austrian Foreign Minister Count Berchtold. Both men believed that Austria needed to punish Serbia. But both men failed to understand that such an action would lead to a wider conflict. Like the crash of a modern jet aircraft—and certainly in keeping with the sinking of the *Titanic*—the outbreak of World War One depended upon a series of failures.

DAY THIRTY. LONDON. JULY 28.

The British ambassador in Berlin sent a telegraph to London with the news that Austria had declared war on Serbia. Once this news reached London, Grey went to the House of Commons. "It must be obvious to any person who reflects on the situation," he told the assembled, "that from the moment the dispute ceases to be one between Austria-Hungary and Serbia and becomes one in which another Great Power is involved, it cannot but end in the greatest catastrophe that has ever befallen the Continent of Europe at one blow."

Unlike Custer and Andrews, Grey had the foresight to see disaster looming dead ahead. What would happen when countries not yet involved in this Balkan conflict began to mobilize? Grey's friend Haldane predicted that the military men would then force the clock to tick according to an irretrievable military timetable.

DAY THIRTY. VIENNA. JULY 28.

In the evening, Foreign Minister Berchtold sent an Austrian declaration of war to the Serbian Foreign Office. The next morning, Austrian artillery units based across the Danube opened fire on the Serbian capital of Belgrade.

DAY THIRTY-ONE. LONDON. JULY 29.

The British Cabinet met two times on this day. A hint of the coming British policy was forwarded to the ambassadors of Germany and France through Grey himself. At the morning meeting, the British Cabinet concluded that a decision regarding a violation of Belgian neutrality, if and when it was made, would be "one of policy rather than legal obligation." In other words, Grey wanted to have all the tools at his disposal to prevent a general war, even if it meant cutting a deal with Germany *after* she had crossed into Belgium's territory. With the noted exception of the Kaiser, Edward Grey was in the best position to use the muscle of his country to prevent just such a war.

Even though Berlin had rejected the six power conference, Grey had not given up hope of working with the principals in Germany. Grey, therefore, called upon Lichnowsky and told him that, even though Berlin had rejected the lead in mediation, he and the British government were prepared to follow Germany in whatever form of mediation she chose. Grey reiterated that he personally felt that Austria had a sincere grievance against Serbia and might even occupy Belgrade as a way to ensure her conditions. An Austrian-Serbian war, he said, would likely graduate to an Austrian-Russian war, but that need not concern Great Britain. If the war was indeed confined to Russia, Serbia, and Austria, Britain might feasibly stand aside. If, however, Germany and France were involved, then Britain's national interests would be at stake and a general war between these great powers would follow.

DAY THIRTY-ONE. BERLIN. JULY 29.

Kaiser Wilhelm and his officials received Lichnowsky's telegram from London containing Grey's remarks. The Germans had a mixed reaction to Grey's warning. The Kaiser grew defensive. Two days earlier, when he scolded his chancellor after returning from vacation, the Kaiser had seemed a man of peace. Now he supported Chancellor Bethmann and seemed willing to risk war. He argued that Grey should direct his venom toward France and Russia.

"He [Grey] knows perfectly well that, if he were to say one single, serious, sharp and warning word at Paris and St. Petersburg, and were to warn them to remain neutral, that both would become quiet at once. But he takes care not to speak the word, and threatens us instead!"

Bethmann believed that Germany's best policy was to keep Britain neutral even though preventing the initial skirmish between Serbia and Austria was no longer possible. Bethmann and the Kaiser agreed that fresh steps must be taken to pacify Edward Grey.

DAY THIRTY-TWO. BERLIN. JULY 30.

In the morning, German Chancellor Bethmann summoned the British ambassador, Edward Goschen, and submitted a proposal to him on the issue of Belgium. "When the war was over, Belgian integrity would be respected if she had not sided against Germany." Bethmann sought Britain's neutrality on the issue of Belgium. Goschen telegraphed the contents to London.

DAY THIRTY-TWO. LONDON. JULY 30.

Grey and his staff were astounded by the German proposal. It seemed to be couched as a bribe or blackmail.

"The document made it clear that Bethmann now thought war probable. Did Bethmann not see that he was making an offer that would dishonor us if we agreed to it? What sort of man was it who could not see that?

Or did he think so badly of us that he thought we should not see it?" Grey had worked for years to keep peace in Europe. His efforts were beginning to unravel in the hands of the Germans and their proposal to go ahead with war, but to "respect Belgian integrity" when the war was over.

"His Majesty's Government cannot for a moment entertain the Chancellor's proposal," Grey responded to Goschen. "It would be a disgrace for us to make this bargain with Germany at the expense of France—a disgrace from which the good name of this country would never recover."

That afternoon, Goschen's telegram containing Bethmann's proposal to keep England neutral and Grey's reply was read to the entire British Cabinet, which, in turn, supported Grey's position on the matter. The term "honor" was beginning, by degrees, to creep into the debate.

DAY THIRTY-TWO. PARIS. JULY 30.

French Foreign Minister Rene Viviani immediately telegraphed Paul Cambon, the French ambassador in London, to remind Grey of the 1912 letter promising that France and England would take "joint steps in the event of tension in Europe." France smelled disaster brewing and immediately commenced a nagging campaign to make sure Britain would fight on the side of France. This was the first of several meetings between Cambon and Grey, each meant to prod England into war. Unfortunately, Grey could not give Cambon the assurance of Britain's support.

DAY THIRTY-TWO. LONDON. JULY 30.

Late in the afternoon, Grey talked privately with Prime Minister Asquith about the problems of a divided Cabinet. Within the British Cabinet was a group of pacifists who absolutely opposed British participation in any continental war. As the prospect of war loomed larger, this group became more active in its determination to keep Britain out. If Grey nudged Britain toward war, these noninterventionists would threaten to resign. Grey's hands were tied. "It was clear to me," he wrote, "that no authority would be obtained from the Cabinet to give the pledge for which France pressed more and more urgently, and that to press the Cabinet for that pledge would be fatal."

DAY THIRTY-TWO. ST. PETERSBURG. JULY 30.

Czar Nicholas II of Russia telegraphed his first cousin, Kaiser Wilhelm II of Germany, during the early morning hours. "Am glad you're back . . . An ignoble war has been declared on a weak country. I believe Belgrade was actually shelled by the Austrians on July 29."

The diplomats from St. Petersburg were growing gloomier and gloomier. The Russian foreign minister, Sazonov, had given every indication that Russia was willing to accommodate some Austrian vindictiveness over the murder of their Archduke as long as Austria allowed Serbia to maintain its sovereign right. His master, Czar Nicholas, was essentially a peace-loving man and, throughout the first days of the crisis, resisted the pleas of his military men to mobilize. The Russian people, however, were more willing to accept the inevitability of war. Under pressure, the Czar signed an order to mobilize Moscow, Kiev, Odessa, and Kazan. Each of these districts contained army corps directed against Austria.

DAY THIRTY-TWO. LONDON. JULY 30.

After dinner, Grey took the opportunity to snatch a few hours sleep. The burden of resolving the crisis had fallen on his shoulders. Unlike Custer, who was youthful and zealous, and unlike Thomas Andrews, who had such little time to contemplate his failure, Grey was plagued by the conflict between his past role as a man of peace and the growing prospect of sending Britain to war.

Grey was fifty-two. He missed the company of his late wife. And now he was gradually going blind. Already he was having difficulty seeing the squash ball. By the spring of 1914 he was having trouble reading. Doctors suggested six months of rest in the country, but Grey refused. Unlike Thomas Andrews and Custer, Grey had no particular love for his job, but he was still devoted to duty and country. During these days in late July and early August, he was subjected to the persistent pleas of Cambon, the French ambassador, and the concerns of Lichnowsky, the German ambassador. This was coupled by the constant demands of the British Cabinet. Telegrams flew back and forth. The demands on Grey amounted to a twenty-four hour barrage.

DAY THIRTY-THREE. ST. PETERSBURG. JULY 31.

The Russian military generals felt that their partial mobilization left Russia unprotected against Germany. In consequence, they pressured Czar Nicholas to sign a total mobilization order. "Think of the responsibility you are asking me to take if I follow your advice," said the Czar to Foreign Minister Sazonov. "Think of what it means to send thousands and thousands of men to their deaths." Finally, the Czar broke down and, in the afternoon, signed the general mobilization order. The German scheme had succeeded. Now Bethmann in Berlin could say that Russia had mobilized first.

DAY THIRTY-THREE. BERLIN. JULY 31.

Kaiser Wilhelm told Chancellor Bethmann that he was convinced Britain would use the crisis as an excuse to attack Germany. His reaction to Grey's warning of two days earlier was telling. Grey had written that a general war would be "the greatest catastrophe the world has ever seen." On the dispatch beside these words, the Kaiser wrote, "That means they are going to attack us." The Germans had assumed that England would stand aside if war broke out between Austria and Serbia. Now, sadly, the Kaiser pinned much of the blame on the British for the snowball his ministers had started rolling. "England alone bears responsibility for peace or war, not we now," wrote the Kaiser later that day. "My work is at an end."

DAY THIRTY-THREE. LONDON. JULY 31.

Late in the afternoon, Grey once again played the Belgium card by sending off dispatches to both France and Germany. He asked that both countries respect Belgian neutrality and that neither country invade Belgian territory unless another major power had already done so.

France, of course, agreed. Germany remained vague and evasive. Jagow told the British ambassador, Edward Goschen, that he would have to consult the Kaiser and the Kaiser's chancellor before responding.

Grey sympathized with France. As July came to a close, and during the course of his muted negotiations with the French ambassador, Paul Cambon, Grey could not imagine Britain watching from across the English Channel while France was caught in a death struggle with Germany. Grey believed that a war would bring unimaginable destruction to the national life and wealth of the countries involved. Once the nations saw this, they must rationally step back from the abyss. In the event of war, Grey saw Britain's long-range interest in supporting France. If a majority of the Cabinet could not accept this view, Grey threatened to resign. During the course of the drama, Grey could make no pledges on behalf of England that the nation might not fulfill.

The French were in a difficult spot. They knew that Germany would attack in a few days. They needed Britain on her side lest the stronger German armies pounded her into submission. Britain, in this case, wore the clothing of Edward Grey, and Cambon and Grey were friends.

On the one hand, it was Cambon's job to push Grey into a commitment; on the other hand, he did not want to push Grey too hard, for if he forced Grey's hand into taking the hard-line stance of military commitment to France no matter what, Grey might provoke a reaction from the Cabinet that would lead to his departure.

Edward Grey went to bed that night filled with apprehension. He reviewed in his mind the events of the preceding month. That night and many nights thereafter, he considered whether he had done everything in his power to prevent the conflagration.

DAY THIRTY-FOUR. ST. PETERSBURG. SATURDAY, AUGUST 1.

The German ambassador to Russia, Count Friederich von Pourtales, arrived for an appointment with the Russian foreign minister, Sergie Sazonov. The count requested a response to the German ultimatum that Russia revoke its mobilization order. When Sazonov refused, Pourtales handed him Germany's declaration of war. Sazonov reviewed its contents. The two men had been friends for years. Now, they were at the brink. Sazonov raised his gaze back to Germany's representative and said, "The curses of nations will be upon you."

A pause. "We are defending our honor," replied Pourtales.

"Your honor was not involved. But there is a divine justice."

Pourtales looked through the open window and muttered, "A divine justice . . . a divine justice." The two men embraced. Pourtales began to weep as they said goodbye.

DAY THIRTY-FOUR. LONDON. SATURDAY, AUGUST 1.

Edward Grey rose early and breakfasted in his office. His most pressing concern was France. Twelve of the eighteen Cabinet ministers opposed going to war on behalf of France. This week a British magazine published lines reflecting the thoughts of an average British citizen:

> Why should I follow your fighting line
> For a matter that's no concern of mine?
> I shall be asked to a general scrap
> All over the European map,
> Dragged into somebody else's war
> For that's what a double entente is for.

Grey sought two things: maximum support of France and an unconditional guarantee of Belgian neutrality. That Saturday, he found neither. Belgian neutrality was the one element the deeply divided British Cabinet could agree upon, but Germany had not yet directly threatened Belgium. Moreover, the British were not sure that Belgium would oppose violation of their soil, and if the Belgians did not fight, the peace group argued, then the British could not commit the nation to war because of a simple transverse over Belgium's soil. In addition, England's businessmen were growing more and more alarmed, fearing that war would hurt Europe's economies. Prime Minister Asquith rebuffed them, "The men of the City are the greatest ninnies I ever had to tackle. I found them all in a state of funk like old women chattering over teacups in a cathedral town."

But Grey was losing time. Each hour mattered. That first day of August he envisioned a continent of Europe teeming with German troops, and he remembered the promises he had made to France. Sitting in that Cabinet meeting, he was forced to listen to Lloyd George claim that any breach of Belgian territory would be just a "little violation." Grey watched as the Liberal party leader traced a short line with his finger across the map of Belgium. When Grey finally had his turn to speak, he proposed immediately implementing the promise that Britain had made to France to use the Royal Navy to defend the coastline of the English Channel. Upon hearing that, four Cabinet ministers—Lord Morely, John Burns, Sir John Simon, and Lewis Harcourt—threatened to resign. War was a vague prospect, they argued, the bare beginnings of a storm on a distant horizon.

Day Thirty-four. Berlin. Saturday, August 1.

Kaiser Wilhelm received a telegram from Ambassador Lichnowsky describing events in London. The Kaiser, to some extent, was still a reluctant warrior. German generals were itching to mobilize, a process that involved thousands of trains and millions of troops. The Schlieffen Plan had been designed with thoroughness and attention to detail. Everything was ready to go, and it was merely a word from the Kaiser that would set the wheels in motion. Wilhelm, however, had other ideas. Still uneasy over the prospect of a two-front war, he reviewed the telegram he just received from Lichnowsky. That morning, in London, during a break in the Cabinet meeting, Grey told Lichnowsky that England would help to keep France neutral if Germany would promise not to attack France or Russia. Lichnowsky interpreted this as an offer to focus on France alone, thus providing the Kaiser with a golden opportunity to avoid a two-front war.

He waved Lichnowsky's telegram at Helmuth von Moltke, commander-in-chief of the German forces. "We simply march the whole army to the East!"

For Moltke, these words were anathema. This tall, heavy-set, balding Prussian had spent nearly his entire adult life training and waiting for *Der Tag*, which means literally "Such Day," a day on which his mentor, Schlieffen, saw no alternative but a two-front war. The plan called for a set of schedules that intricately tied together details of launching troop trains both east and west. Although not necessarily confident about the ultimate outcome of the war, Moltke was nevertheless determined to launch it according to a plan that was twenty years in the making and that had been worked over, detail by detail, by obsessive German generals.

"Your Majesty," Moltke said, "it cannot be done. The deployment of millions cannot be improvised. If Your Majesty insists on leading the whole army to the East it will not be any army ready for battle but a disorganized mob of armed men with no arrangements for supply." The arrangements for deployment that the generals had already made had taken them a whole year to devise.

Kaiser Wilhelm glowered at him. "Your uncle would have given me a different answer." (He was referring to Germany's great Field Marshall Moltke).

The two men parted with the Kaiser still determined to turn his army to the east and Moltke just as determined to initiate the Schlieffen Plan as it was. On what should have been the penultimate day of his career, Moltke returned to his general staff headquarters and burst into tears. When an aide later brought the Kaiser's written orders that canceled the western movement of his troops, Moltke took his pen from his coat pocket and threw it on the table. "Do what you want with this telegram; I will not sign it."

Moltke was still brooding when another summons came from the palace. There, Moltke found the Kaiser in his bedroom wearing his military clothing over his nightshirt. Another telegram had arrived from Lichnowsky, who, in a further conversation with Grey, had discovered the "mistake" he had made earlier, referring to the deliberate misinformation he had conveyed to the Kaiser about Grey/Britain's intentions regarding France and Russia. Now, in this latest telegram, Lichnowsky told Berlin conclusively, "A positive proposal by England is, on the whole, not in prospect."

"Now you can do what you like," said the Kaiser to his general before going back to bed.

Moltke now had the orders he desired. Still, he was shaken. Referring to his initial failure to persuade the Kaiser, Moltke later wrote, "That was my first experience of the war. I never recovered from the shock of this incident. Something in me broke and I was never the same thereafter."

Day Thirty-four. London. Saturday, August 1.

Early in the afternoon, German Ambassador Lichnowsky met with Grey. In their discussion, Grey clarified his earlier statement regarding Britain's intentions. "England would keep France neutral if Germany promised not to attack France *and* Russia." Perhaps earlier Lichnowsky had heard only what he wanted to hear, that Grey would keep France out of the war if Germany attacked only Russia. But Germany was set on a two-front war she thought she could win. All the planning and the training which had underscored the lives of two generations of Prussian military men was about to be set in motion. From the moment the Kaiser had said to Moltke, "Now you can do what you like," the Schlieffen Plan in all its intricacy began to roll. Millions of men, eleven thousand trains, tons of supplies and ammunition along with the staffs of companies, officers, and division staffs began the march east and west. That night, Germany violated the Luxemburg border when an infantry company of the 69th regiment, commanded by a certain Lieutenant Feldman, took over a town called Trois Vierges (Three Virgins).

Certainly, the French bore no illusions about the intent of the German plan. For French Ambassador Paul Cambon in particular, it was now a question of bringing England into a war the French knew they were going to fight. That same afternoon, Cambon found a single, precious moment to press Edward Grey for a commitment. "France must take her own decision at this moment," said Grey, "without reckoning on an assistance we are not now in a position to give." Grey was, of course, waiting for the violation of Belgian neutrality by the Germans—the event which he felt would unify the British Cabinet for war—before he could give France any commitments. But Grey's comment nevertheless stung Cambon. When an editor of *The Times of London* asked Cambon what he was going to do, Cambon replied, "I am going to wait to learn if the word 'honor' should be erased from the English dictionary."

That evening Germany declared war on Russia. Grey told Cambon that England would not allow the German fleet to enter the English Channel.

DAY THIRTY-FIVE. LONDON. SUNDAY, AUGUST 2.

The British Cabinet reconvened at eleven in the morning. Grey addressed his fellow Cabinet Ministers, "We could not stand the sight of the German Fleet coming down the Channel and, within sight and sound of our shores, bombing the French coast." Therefore, he intended to make official what he had promised the night before, that Britain would allow Churchill to dispatch the fleet to protect the Channel, a move warlike enough to force at least two ministers from the peace group to resign. Earlier in the day, Lichnowsky had come to see Asquith and had pleaded with him to keep his country out of the war. "We have no desire to intervene," Asquith told him, "but Germany must not send her fleet into the Channel to attack France and she must not, I repeat must not, invade Belgium."

DAY THIRTY-FIVE. BRUSSELS. SUNDAY, AUGUST 2.

The German minister in the Belgian capital was advised to open a sealed envelope that he had received on July 29 and then deliver the contents of that envelope to the Belgian government. Because the Schlieffen Plan called for decisive victory through speed, the quickest way to get the German armies into the heart of France was through Belgium. No other route would do. After the German minister handed the note to his Belgian counterpart, the higher-ups in this small, neutral country gathered at their foreign office and listened to what amounted to a thinly disguised ultimatum, which read:

> Germany had reliable information of a proposed advance by the French along the route Giver-Namur leaving no doubt of France's intention to advance against Germany through Belgian territory. Germany, being unable to count on the Belgian Army halting the French advance, required the dictate of self-preservation to anticipate this hostile attack. She would view with deepest regret if Belgium should regard her entrance on Belgian soil as an act of hostility against herself. If Belgium should, on the other hand, adopt a benevolent neutrality, Germany would bind herself to evacuate her territory as soon as peace shall have been concluded, to pay for any damages caused by German troops, and to guarantee at the conclusion of peace the sovereign rights and independence of the kingdom. If

Belgium opposed Germany's passage through her territory she would be regarded as an enemy and future relations with her would be left to the decision of arms. Germany demands an unequivocal answer in twelve hours.

"What does he take me for?" exclaimed young King Albert I upon hearing the ultimatum. "Our answer must be 'No' whatever the consequences. Our duty is to defend our territorial integrity. In this we must not fail." His ministers agreed. The Belgians knew the consequences of their decision—the German army would destroy the country—but the honor of their people was at stake and they did not equivocate.

Day Thirty-five. London. Sunday, August 2.

The British Cabinet met for a second time at six-thirty in the evening, unaware of the German ultimatum to Belgium. The war group—consisting of Churchill, Balfour, Haldane, Grey, and others—expressed deep concern that a German victory over France would mean Berlin's dominance over all of continental Europe. Unfortunately, England's support for France had never been fully made clear to the British public and many members of the Liberal government did not accept it.

In other words, many English subjects saw the crisis as just another quarrel in an old conflict between Germany and France. Thus, Grey was still facing the dilemma of his country heading into war divided. Only the violation of Belgian neutrality—in direct contravention to a British treaty—would convince the peace group that war was necessary. Grey was determined to ask the Cabinet the next morning to regard the German invasion of Belgium as a formal *casus belli*.

That evening, as Grey and his friend, Richard Haldane, were having dinner, a box was brought to Grey with a telegram inside confirming the German ultimatum to Belgium. Grey and Haldane left dinner and drove to 10 Downing Street where they showed the note to Asquith. All three men agreed that the German ultimatum to Belgium—with invasion to follow—meant the least they should do was mobilize the British armed forces.

Day Thirty-six. London. Monday, August 3.

Edward Grey awakened to a fistful of telegrams from all over the world. He had fallen asleep in his office the night before trying to compose notes for a speech to Parliament. Now this day—a banking holiday—dawned clear and beautiful. From eleven in the morning until two in the afternoon he sat through a hectic Cabinet meeting during which the ministers learned that Belgium intended to defend her country.

Seven German armies totaling a million-and-a-half men stood at the French and Belgian borders. From the moment Moltke got things started, these troops began rolling west, carrying sabers, pistols, rifles, and twelve-foot, steel-headed lances. Against the German forces, Belgium had six small divisions of troops, approximately 120,000 men.

DAY THIRTY-SIX. RIVER MEUSE. MONDAY, AUGUST 3.

Brigades under the command of German General von Emmich found the bridges across the River Meuse destroyed. When his troops attempted to cross the river on hastily erected pontoons, Belgian sharpshooters on the far bank opened fire. The Germans, who never expected to meet serious resistance until they faced the French, were now surprised to discover live ammunition hurled at them and appalled to see their men bleeding to death in the river.

DAY THIRTY-SIX. LONDON. 2:00 PM. MONDAY, AUGUST 3.

Working at the Foreign Office to prepare his speech for Parliament, Grey was interrupted by German Ambassador Lichnowsky, who implored Grey not to name the invasion of Belgium as a condition on which Britain would enter the war. "Moltke's troops may cut through only a very small corner of the country," Lichnowsky said. "Need that be a reason to fight?" But Grey said that he could not reveal the contents of his speech. The two men, friends for years, talked in Grey's doorway for half-an-hour. Although Lichnowsky would have waited an eternity to retrieve a few morsels of hope from his friend, Grey would not help him. Germans were already crossing into Belgium. The speech Grey had to write pressed on him. The two men said a last goodbye and parted.

DAY THIRTY-SIX. LONDON. 3:00 PM. MONDAY, AUGUST 3.

Minutes before Grey was to deliver his epochal address to Parliament, the crowd was so thick on the street between the Foreign Office and the Houses of Parliament that Grey needed a police escort to make his way through. He entered the chamber wearing a light summer suit. According to one commentator, he looked "extraordinarily pale, with curious redness, of nights without sleep, too much reading and writing, around the eyes." Churchill and Asquith entered, and all took their seats on the Treasury Bench.

As he sat waiting to deliver the most important speech of his life, Grey may well have thought back to an earlier time, the days when he was newly wedded to a wife whom he loved. He remembered when, as a new member of Parliament, he had listened to Prime Minister Gladstone introduce his first Home Rule Bill to a crowded House of Commons. Recalling the road he traveled—the early death of a beloved wife and now the certain prospect of general war—Grey almost broke down. Yet when the Speaker called his name, he rose and addressed the House. "I do not recall feeling nervous," he remembered later. "At such a moment there could be neither hope of personal success nor fear of personal failure. In a great crisis, a man who has to act or speak stands bare and stripped of choice. He has to do what is in him to do."

Grey's speech to Parliament that day was a milestone. Participants remember a clear, dignified, unadorned speech by a man who had for the duration of his career dreaded being placed in exactly this pivotal position. He did not relish action, as Churchill did, nor did he gravitate to the company of men. To be the gatekeeper before the path of war was a position in which Grey never wanted to find himself, and yet he had to galvanize a divided country to armed conflict.

He told the House to approach this crisis from the viewpoint of British interests, British honor, and British obligation. He first mentioned the military conversations with France that had taken place behind closed doors for years, noting that these unofficial arrangements did not bind Britain into a war for the benefit of France. France had entered the war because of her "obligation of honor to Russia but we are not parties to the Franco-Russian alliance; we do not even know the terms of that alliance." He then discussed the naval arrangements with France. "It is my feeling that if the German Fleet came down the Channel and bombarded and battered the undefended coast of France, we could not stand aside and see this going on practically within sight of our eyes, with our arms folded, looking on dispassionately, doing nothing."

When the cheers died down, Grey resumed, focusing on British trade routes and British interests before moving to the subject of British neutrality, the linchpin of his speech.

> I ask the House from the point of view of British interests to consider what may be at stake. If France is beaten to her knees . . . if Belgium fell under the same dominating influence and then Holland and then Denmark . . . if, in a crisis like this, we run away from these obligations of honor and

interest as regards the Belgian Treaty . . . I do not believe for a moment at the end of this war, even if we stood aside, we should be unable to undo what had happened, in the course of the war, to prevent the whole of the west of Europe opposite us from falling under the domination of a single power . . . and we should, I believe, sacrifice our respect and good name and reputation before the world and should not escape the most serious and grave economic consequences . . . Could this country stand by and witness the direst crime that ever stained the pages of history and thus become particpators in the sin? I ask for your support at this grave hour not only by the House of Commons, but by the determination and the resolution, the courage and endurance of the whole country.

Grey spoke for an hour and fifteen minutes. He was interrupted by applause and cheers throughout his speech. With little time to prepare, he had delivered the speech of his life. He had unified a divided nation and prepared it for war.

Peace had failed. Although the experts predicted this war would only last a few months, it went on for four years. Nine million men died and twice that many were wounded—and this would only be the beginning. Winston Churchill saw both world wars as a "single continuing Great War running through the whole of the middle of the Twentieth Century." It was as if 1914 to 1945 was another Thirty Years' War.

Winston Churchill accompanied Grey as the two men left the House of Commons. "What happens now?" asked Churchill.

"Now" replied Grey, "we shall send them [the Germans] an ultimatum to stop the invasion of Belgium within twenty-four hours."

In the German camp there was one Austrian in particular who gleefully accepted the coming of war. A photograph catches this young man cheering with the crowds in Munich two days before Grey's speech. Twenty-five-year-old Adolph Hitler came of age in the Great War. His experience in World War One would shape the conflict that followed twenty years later.

Unlike Hitler, Edward Grey represented the best of Western man. His belief and adherence to duty; his love of nature and literature—what a contrast to Custer, who brought death to Indian women and children on the American Plains, or those Germans who engineered and executed the invasion of Belgium. Many of the seeds of atrocity that bore fruit in World War Two were sown in Germany's western invasion of that neutral country.

That August of 1914 saw Belgian civilians—men, women, and children—rounded up in town squares and shot by German soldiers. Those not dead from gunfire were bayoneted, including infants. An ancient library in the Belgian city of Louvain was set ablaze, even though the Germans knew it contained a priceless and irreplaceable collection. The killing—a procedure the Germans would institutionalize in the next war—began in earnest in 1914. Five thousand humans sacrificed their lives on an average day to the maniacal German plan devised by Schlieffen and opposed by Grey. All this death erased an old language. As Ernest Hemingway wrote, "Abstract words such as glory, honor, courage, or hallow were obscene beside the concrete names of villages, the number of roads, the names of rivers, the numbers of regiments and the dates."

DAY THIRTY-SIX. LONDON. 7:00 PM. MONDAY, AUGUST 3.

When Edward Grey returned to the Foreign Office that Monday evening after his speech, he received the American ambassador, Walter Page. The two men talked in hushed tones.

When Page asked if Germany would agree to pull back her troops from Belgium, Grey shook his head. "No, of course everybody knows there will be war." He stopped for a moment and struggled for words. Like the hero of Wallace Stevens's poem, "Tea at the Palaz of Hoon," Grey had "found himself more truly and more strange" as he descended the western day, as if in reaching this point of despair he finally came to understand himself. It was at this moment, too, that Grey found his epiphany, the sudden illumination of inalterably changed circumstances—just as Custer had found his in the moment he saw the size of the Indian village—just as Thomas Andrews found his upon inspecting the damage to the *Titanic's* hull. When Grey resumed speaking, his eyes were filled with tears. "Thus, the efforts of a lifetime go for nothing," he said, "I feel like a man who has wasted his life."

But, of course, his life was not wasted. Grey stands alone, as the last man of the Nineteenth Century. He had kept the peace for as long as he possibly could and then, when war came, he made sure Britain entered it united.

The Twentieth Century—that preposterous, hectic, bloody century—was set in motion the first days of August 1914. Since then we've had little rest, little peace.

Watching with a friend at his window of the Foreign Office as the street lamps were being lit below, Grey spoke the final words of the drama with an understatement that foreshadowed all that was to come. "The lamps are going out all over Europe," he said. "We shall not see them lit again in our lifetime."

APPENDIX

NOTES

Part One
The Strange Ride of George Custer

Pg. 20 "For all time": Connell, 82.
Pg. 21 "The likelihood that all three columns": Welch, 113.
Pg. 22 "Now, Custer, don't be greedy": Connell, 259.
Pg. 22 "When we return, I will go back to Washington": Connell, 259.
Pg. 23 "I selected him as my game": Connell, 110.
Pg. 23 "Stripped of the beautiful romance": Custer, 21-22.
Pg. 25 "His manner and tone": Graham, 135.
Pg. 25 "Consulted the reports of the commissioner of Indian Affairs": Graham, 134.
Pg. 28 "Here's where Reno made the mistake of his life": Sandoz, 33.
Pg. 28 "He had six troops of cavalry": Sandoz, 33.
Pg. 28 "Go ahead in your own way": Connell, 180.
Pg. 29 "A slaughter pen": Connell, 187.
Pg. 29-30 "If a village is attacked": Wooster, 136.
Pg. 31 "I guess we'll get through with them in one day": Graham, 136.
Pg. 31 "Thieves trail": Welch, 82.
Pg. 31 "Chief of thieves": Welch, 82.
Pg. 34 "Camp at the mouth of the Rosebud River": Graham, 132-33.
Pg. 34-35 "The President of the United States agreed": Stewart, 71-72.
Pg. 35 "Referring to our communications of the 27th": Welch, 53.
Pg. 36 "Wars are too serious": Karnow, 342.
Pg. 36 "Just let me get elected": Karnow, 342.
Pg. 36 "There are many, many people": Karnow, 343.
Pg. 36 "Looking back, US political and military specialists": Karnow, 17.
Pg. 37 "Said Indians are hereby turned over": Ambrose, 397.
Pg. 37 "Farming out": Stewart, 121.
Pg. 38 "I have seen your order transmitted": Stewart, 135.
Pg. 39 "To cut loose from": Stewart, 138.
Pg. 39 "Got away from Stanley": Stewart, 138.
Pg. 39 "I still can't see them": Connell, 269.
Pg. 40 "If Custer had come up": Connell, 414.

Pg. 40 "We asked him to raise his hand": Connell, 415.

Pg. 40 "Their hearts strong": Stewart, 280-281.

Pg. 41 "I shall not see you go": Stewart, 316.

Pg. 41 "The largest Indian Camp": Ambrose, 431.

Pg. 41 "You and I are both going home": Connell, 274.

Pg. 43 "The brass hats are to blame": Connell, 15.

Pg. 44 "Here go your Indians": Stewart, 324.

Pg. 44 "The village was only two miles above": Graham, 139.

Pg. 45 "Or whatever it may be called": Connell, 404.

Pg. 45 "Benteen. Come on. Big village.": Graham, 142.

Part Two

The Short, Happy Life of Thomas Andrews

Pg. 50 "I cannot conceive any condition": Lord, *Night Lives On*, 28.

Pg. 50 "Captain, *Titanic*": Merideth, 120.

Pg. 52 "Practically unsinkable": Kuntz, 33.

Pg. 52 "Captain Smith, *Titanic*": Lynch, 66.

Pg. 53 "We are not going": Lynch, 74.

Pg. 53 "I expect around": Lynch, 76.

Pg. 55 "What is the name": Wade, 202.

Pg. 56 "The corner": Lynch, 74.

Pg. 56 "From *Mesaba* to *Titanic*": Winocour, 71-72.

Pg. 57 "Casually": Lord, Night Lives On, 63.

Pg. 58 "Chances of favorable outcome": Janis, 78.

Pg. 58 "This dispatch is to be": Janis, 78.

Pg. 59 "She was a brilliant woman": Janis, 76.

Pg. 59 "The Japanese could not": Janis, 82-83.

Pg. 59 "We finally decided": Janis, 83.

Pg. 60 "What, you don't know": Janis, 91.

Pg. 60 "It would have been": Prange, 516.

Pg. 61 "He was a great favorite": Winocour, 275.

Pg. 61 "Yes, it is very cold": Lord, *Night Lives On*, 64.

Pg. 61-62 "If it becomes at all": Lord, *Night Lives On*, 65.

Pg. 62 "It defied my understanding": Vaughan, 48.

Pg. 63 "The attention paid to managers": Vaughan, 66.

Pg. 63 "According to Emerson's rule": Tuchman, *Practicing History*, 75.

Pg. 64 "Looked like something": Vaughan, 330.

Pg. 64 "We were absolutely relentless": Vaughan, 221.

Pg. 64 "With all procedural systems": Vaughan, 347.

Pg. 65 "It is very cold": Lynch, 79.

Pg. 65 "It is pretty cold": Lynch, 82.

Pg. 65 "We might be": Lynch, 82.

Pg. 65 "Shut up. Shut up.": Kuntz, 326.

Pg. 66 "We're looking for": NTSB/AAR-99/01,3.
Pg. 67 "We reached here": Bullock, 62.
Pg. 67 "Just wouldn't retire": Lord, *Night Lives On*, 1
Pg. 68 "Hard a' port": Lynch, 89.
Pg. 68 "What have we struck?": Lynch, 89.
Pg. 69 "The connection to Lord Pirrie": Bullock, 1.
Pg. 70 "One sees him": Bullock, 21.
Pg. 70 "What we think": Bullock, 35.
Pg. 71 "The ship is making water": Lynch, 91.
Pg. 71 "Is the damage serious?": Lynch, 92.
Pg. 71 "We have struck ice": Kuntz, 3.
Pg. 75 "Aircraft parts": Langewiesche, 211.
Pg. 75 "Oxygen canisters-empty": Langewiesche, 211.
Pg. 76 "That were expired": Langewiesche, 228.
Pg. 76 "Were not expended": Langewiesche, 228.
Pg. 76 "All serviceable and": Langewiesche, 230-31.
Pg. 76 "An expended oxygen": Langewiesche, 231.
Pg. 78 "What was the full": Kuntz, 22.
Pg. 78 "I could not tell": Kuntz, 22.
Pg. 78 "What was that?": Langewiesche, 212.
Pg. 79 "I need a supervisor": Langewiesche, 199.
Pg. 79 "Critter five-ninety-two": Langewiesche, 201.
Pg. 80 "Critter five-ninety-two, you can": Langewiesche, 201.
Pg. 80 "Critter fiver-ninety-two, Opa-locka": Langewiesche, 202.
Pg. 80 "At first we did not realize": Bullock, 66-67.
Pg. 81 "There was peace": Thayer, 8.
Pg. 82 "Aren't you going": Bullock, 73.

Part Three
The Last Man of the Nineteenth Century

Pg. 86 "Come to think": Robbins, 131.
Pg. 86 "When I was sent down": Trevelyan, 23.
Pg. 87 "So you read": Trevelyan, 21-22.
Pg. 88 "The blackness of town life": Robbins, 45.
Pg. 88 "There is an aspect of London": Robbins, 72.
Pg. 88 "There is the aggressive stiffness": Robbins, 72.
Pg. 88 "My wife and I": Robbins, 71.
Pg. 88-89 "My holiday was wrecked": Robbins, 209.
Pg. 89 "Be bold, be bold": Tuchman, *Guns of August*, 26.
Pg. 89 "The great battle of France": Keegan, 370-371.
Pg. 90 "A heavily one-sided": Tuchman, *Guns of August*, 21.
Pg. 90 "When you march": Tuchman, *Guns of August*, 25.
Pg. 91 "A victory on the battlefield": Tuchman, *Guns of August*, 396.

Pg. 91 "Plain common sense": Tuchman, *Guns of August*, 23.

Pg. 91 "It must come to a fight": Tuchman, *Guns of August*, 25.

Pg. 92 "The death of Mother": Robbins, 153.

Pg. 92 "This week is worse": Robbins, 154.

Pg. 92 "The Germans do not realize": Robbins, 155.

Pg. 93 "If some member": Cassels, 38.

Pg. 93 "We are all constantly": Cassels, 162.

Pg. 93 "They are shooting us": Taylor, 19.

Pg. 93 "Is worse off": Cassels, 72.

Pg. 94 "Are paradoxically the only friends": Taylor, 1.

Pg. 94 "Krajina's like a blood-soaked rag": Cassels, 75.

Pg. 96 "The wet logs on the open fire": Cassels, 76.

Pg. 96 "The Serbian soul": Cassels, 76.

Pg. 96 "Vampires and oppressors": Cassels, 7.

Pg. 96 "To identify themselves": Cassels, 7.

Pg. 98 "One day Tankosic": Cassels, 149.

Pg. 99 "Look after these men": Cassels, 150.

Pg. 102 "Rather strangely dressed": Cassels, 174.

Pg. 102 "When I saw the Archduke": Cassels, 174.

Pg. 103 "So, I come here on a state visit": Taylor 10.

Pg. 103 "Your imperial and royal Highness": Brook-Shepherd, 248.

Pg. 103 "What, do you think": Taylor, 10.

Pg. 103 "I assure you": Taylor, 10.

Pg. 104 "In God's name": Cassels, 179.

Pg. 104 "Sophie! Sophie!": Cassels, 179.

Pg. 104 "Do you think I am an animal?": Cassels, 193.

Pg. 104 "*Es ist nichts*": Cassels, 179.

Pg. 104 "I am not a criminal": Cassels, 193.

Pg. 104 "A higher power": Gilbert, 17.

Pg. 104 "No crime": Massie, 860.

Pg. 107 "Nothing has been spared me": Cassels, 38.

Pg. 107 "The crime against my nephew": Massie, 861.

Pg. 107 "Count on Germany's": Massie, 861.

Pg. 107 "Russia is in no way": Massie, 861.

Pg. 107 "The views of the Kaiser": Massie, 862.

Pg. 108 "When, as a little boy": Massie, 151.

Pg. 108 "You see that man": Tuchman, *Guns of August*, 106.

Pg. 108 "Only fit to live": Tuchman, *Guns of August*, 8.

Pg. 108 "My advice to you": Tuchman, *Guns of August*, 8-9.

Pg. 108 "I hate the Slavs": Tuchman, *Guns of August*, 73-74.

Pg. 109 "Had come to London": Tuchman, *Guns of August*, 77.

Pg. 109 "Spoke English and copied": Tuchman, *Guns of August*, 77.

Pg. 109 "German government are": Robbins, 292.

Pg. 110 "England wished to preserve": Robbins, 293.

Pg. 110 "Had been endeavoring": Gilbert, 20.

Pg. 110 "I have my doubts": Gilbert, 20.

Pg. 110 "An alley of bomb throwers": Taylor, 11.

Pg. 111 "The note is being composed": Massie, 864.

Pg. 111 "To avoid alarming": Massie, 864.

Pg. 112 "We should consider it unwise": Massie, 865.

Pg. 112 "The most formidable document": Massie, 866.

Pg. 112 "Some damn foolish thing": Tuchman, *Guns of August*, 71.

Pg. 113 "The discussion had reached": Churchill 100-101.

Pg. 115 "Part of your demands": Taylor, 215.

Pg. 115 "If our respective governments": Grey, Vol I, 304.

Pg. 116 "Sir E. Grey had me call": Massie, 882.

Pg. 116 "How did it all happen?": Massie, 869.

Pg. 116 "No, you've cooked this": Massie, 869.

Pg. 117 "A brilliant performance": Massie, 869.

Pg. 117 "Avoid very carefully": Massie, 869.

Pg. 118 "It must be obvious": Massie, 883.

Pg. 118 "One of policy": Massie, 884.

Pg. 119 "He knows perfectly well": Massie, 887.

Pg. 119 "When the war was over": Massie, 887.

Pg. 119 "The document made it clear": Massie, 888.

Pg. 120 "His Majesty's Government": Massie, 888.

Pg. 120 "Joint steps in the event": Massie, 889.

Pg. 120 "It was clear to me": Massie, 889.

Pg. 120 "Am glad you're back": Massie, 869.

Pg. 121 "Think of the responsibility": Taylor, 34.

Pg. 122 "The greatest catastrophe": Taylor, 224.

Pg. 122 "That means they are going": Massie, 886.

Pg. 122 "England alone bears": Taylor, 225.

Pg. 123 "The curses of nations": Tuchman, *Guns of August*, 83.

Pg. 123 "Why should I follow": Tuchman, *Guns of August*, 92.

Pg. 124 "The men of the City": Massie, 899.

Pg. 124 "Little violation": Massie, 887.

Pg. 125 "We simply march": Tuchman, *Guns of August*, 78.

Pg. 125 "Your Majesty": Tuchman, *Guns of August*, 79.

Pg. 125 "Do what you want": Tuchman, *Guns of August*, 81.

Pg. 126 "A positive proposal by England": Tuchman, *Guns of August*, 81.

Pg. 126 "That was my first experience": Tuchman, *Guns of August*, 81-82.

Pg. 126 "England would keep France": Grey, Vol II, 329.

Pg. 126 "France must take her own": Tuchman, *Guns of August*, 96.

Pg. 126 "I am going to wait": Tuchman, *Guns of August*, 96.

Pg. 127 "We could not stand the sight": Massie, 900.

Pg. 127 "We have no desire": Massie, 901.

Pg. 127 "Germany had reliable information": Tuchman, *Guns of August*, 101-102.

Pg. 128 "What does he take me for?": Tuchman, *Guns of August*, 108.

Pg. 129 "Moltke's troops may cut": Massie, 903.

Pg. 129 "Extraordinarily pale": Massie, 904.

Pg. 130 "I do not recall feeling nervous": Grey, Vol II, 14.

Pg. 130 "Obligation of honor": Grey, Vol II, 313.

Pg. 130 "It is my feeling": Grey, Vol II, 314.

Pg. 130-131 "I ask the House": Grey, Vol. II, 321-322.

Pg. 131 "Single continuing Great War": Churchill, 7.

Pg. 131 "What happens now?": Churchill, 120.

Pg. 132 "Abstract words such as glory": Hemingway, 185.

Pg. 132 "No, of course, everybody knows": Massie, 907.

Pg. 132 "Found himself more truly": Stevens, 65.

Pg. 132 "Thus, the efforts of a lifetime": Massie, 907.

Pg. 133 "The lamps are going out": Grey, Vol II, 20.

Comments on Notes

Comment (from page 58): The issues arising from the Pearl Harbor tragedy illuminate just how difficult it is to assess the *quality* of warnings.

Given that catastrophe arises from a *series* of failures, one of the elements of that series is a failure to properly assess warnings. However, the circumstances faced by the officers at Pearl Harbor as well as by the officers of the *Titanic* meant that taking action given the warnings that were before them would have been more extraordinary than simply following the course they chose to take. In both cases, the men were forced to consider the warnings from the vantage point of their experience up until that point (without having the luxury of hindsight).

Both Captain Smith and Admiral Kimmel did not, for reasons of efficiency, adopt a worst-case scenario outlook in dealing with the messages they received. In terms of warnings, the catastrophe of September 11th presents many parallels to Pearl Harbor and the *Titanic*. The FBI received two concrete warnings of the September 11th plot during the summer of 2001. In the first, FBI agent Ken Williams sent headquarters a memorandum about Middle Eastern students at an Arizona flight school, theorizing al Qaeda could be using them for a plot to hijack domestic airliners. In the second warning, instructors at a flight school in Minneapolis reported their suspicions about one of their students, Zacarias Moussaoui.

Moussaoui was arrested on immigration charges, but lower level FBI agents were denied permission by their superiors to obtain a special warrant to search his belongings. As late as August 23, 2001, the CIA retrieved old information about a terrorist meeting in Malaysia and asked that two eventual September 11th hijackers, Khalid al-Midhar and Nawaf al-Hazmi, be put on the State Department's watch list for denial of visas. Unfortunately, at that time, they were already in the United States, and an FBI manhunt didn't turn them up before the attacks. In all three instances, the warnings presented officials with the threads of a plot.

Nevertheless, the FBI (and for that matter the CIA) were forced to sift through numerous warnings during the summer of 2001—what National Security Advisor

Condoleezza Rice called "a lot of chatter"—and determining that suspicious Arabic men at American flight schools meant a domestic hijacking plot was too remote to act upon. As Robert L. Bartley wrote in the December 3, 2001 *Wall Street Journal,* "So, too, Osama bin Laden had openly proclaimed *Jihad* against the United States, and his al Qaeda terrorists had repeatedly struck at Americans. They even made a previous attempt at their principal September 11th target. I remember a high official telling me 'we haven't heard the last' of bin Laden. But no one imagined terrorists would have the audacity to hijack airliners and ram them into the twin towers."

Imagination, or actually the failure of imagination, was a subject discussed in Chapter Eleven (Foresight—And Hindsight) of *The 9/11 Commission Report.* One of the principal lessons arising from this report—and how this ties into the Custer, *Titanic,* and World War One stories—is to examine historical events carefully to determine what warnings are relevant. In illuminating the events leading up to the Battle of The Little Bighorn, the sinking of the *Titanic,* and the opening of World War One, we hope to give our readers a greater sense of discrimination in assessing the quality of the warnings that preceded the event. Of course, in this book we are writing with the privilege of hindsight—a benefit that the 9/11 commissioners found to also be a handicap to their analysis. They found the events leading up to 9/11 so salient that they were concerned about missing the nuances of smaller details—"the path of what happened is so brightly lit that it places everything else more deeply in shadow." They, too, noted Pearl Harbor as a model failure in assessing the quality of warnings and cited Roberta Wohlstetter's 1962 book on the subject where she wrote that it is "much easier after the event to sort the relevant from the irrelevant signals. After the event, of course, a signal is always crystal clear; we can now see what disaster it was signaling since the disaster has occurred. But before the event it is obscure and pregnant with conflicting meanings."

In other words, the official who is to decide the course of an action must first sort out what signals are relevant and leave behind those which are irrelevant. Then the official must incorporate his discrimination (informed by his own personal history or otherwise) to determine the importance of those relevant signals. He must, as it were, place them into a hierarchy. In addition to this, he must believe that a particular danger is compelling. Captain Smith, of course, failed this first threshold. He did not believe that an upcoming ice field in the North Atlantic represented a serious danger to his ship. Otherwise, he would have slowed his ship down. Both Presidents Clinton and Bush understood in an intellectual way that bin Laden represented a danger, but "given the character and pace of their policy efforts, we do not believe they fully understood just how many people al Qaeda might kill, and how soon it might do it. At some level that is hard to define, we believe the threat had not yet become compelling."

Even if the threat had become compelling, officials in Washington lacked the imagination to foresee that commercial airliners could be hijacked and used as a fuel-loaded missile to crash into American skyscrapers. Counterterrorism expert Richard Clarke, who worked in both the Clinton and Bush administrations, said that he thought that issuing a warning about the possibility of a suicide hijacking would have been just one more speculative theory among many, hard to spot since the volume of warnings of "al Qaeda threats and other terrorist threats, was in the tens of thousands—probably hundreds of thousands." Yet certain members of the FAA's Civil Aviation Security Intelligence Office foresaw that a suicide hijacking might be an "option of last resort." (Last resort because such an action would not offer al Qaeda an opportunity for dialogue in order to get their colleagues released from American or Israeli prisons.) Of course, even if a government agency had speculated about various scenarios, "the challenge was to flesh out and test those scenarios, then figure out a way to turn scenarios into constructive action." Clarke told the Commission that he was concerned about the danger posed by aircraft in the context of protecting the Atlanta Olympic Games of 1996, the White House complex, and the 2001 G-8 summit in Genoa. "But he attributed his awareness more to Tom Clancy novels than to warnings from the intelligence community. He did not, or could not, press the government to work on the systemic issues of how to strengthen the layered security defenses to protect aircraft against hijackings or put the adequacy of air defenses against suicide hijackers on the national policy agenda."

How do you teach imagination? Custer certainly had the experience to fully appreciate the potential dangers of attacking an Indian village filled with hostile Sioux and Cheyenne warriors, but he did not have the imagination to foresee just how many warriors would counterattack or that their collective motivation would be so deadly. Thomas Andrews was fully aware that he could design a ship with more enhanced safety features than he implemented into the *Titanic*, but he did not imagine that his ship might strike a rock, another ship, or an iceberg that might puncture the hull at points beyond the junction of two watertight compartments. Edward Grey, on the hand, could imagine the terrible loss of life that might result from a general European war, but he lacked imagination to foresee that his policy of "balancing European powers" against one another might set into place a potential chain reaction of warring countries.

The critical issue is to foresee the pathway to disaster before the chain reaction of events becomes irreversible. In the case of the 9/11 disaster (unlike Pearl Harbor), the commissioners found that the relevant signals may have been too obscure or diffuse to see any pattern by which to act. Richard Clarke told the Commission that his policy advice to the Bush administration, "even if it had been accepted immediately and turned into action, would not have prevented 9/11." Moreover, sometimes the threat does not seem compelling enough to warrant the kind of severe action it would take to prevent disaster. For example, overthrowing the Taliban regime in Afghanistan would have eliminated bin Laden's sanctuary, but to do so would have meant direct military actions of some sort (a land invasion or air attacks), and those approaches "must have seemed—if they were considered at all—to be disproportionate to the threat."

The key is to examine historical events carefully. An official needs to consider what signals from a particular historical example might bear some resemblance to the pattern of signals arising from the problem at hand. Do recurring warnings of icebergs bear any resemblance to repeated warnings of the movements of the

Japanese fleet in the Pacific Ocean or to warnings that critical rubber O-rings show noticeable erosion after each space shuttle launch?

Sometimes the patterns seem so close and obvious that one wonders why preventive action hadn't been taken before. For example, the giant tsunami that swept across the Indian Ocean in late December 2004 killed over 150,000 people. One commentator noted, "As diplomatic warnings filtered slowly around bureaucratic channels across Asia that Sunday morning, fishermen set out in flimsy boats, children splashed in the waves and tourists escaping winter climates lay out on beaches or went snorkeling amid the coral. Unbeknownst to them, a tsunami of Biblical proportions, created by one of the largest undersea earthquakes in decades, was speeding across the Indian Ocean. . . This was also a failure of imagination—the inability of dozens of experts and officials in a score of countries to fathom that an undersea earthquake could conceivably cause such havoc, so far away." Had that tsunami occurred in the Pacific Ocean, the loss of life would have been far less. Why? Because many countries in the Pacific Rim pay for and participate in an early warning system for tsunamis. Such a system was not in place for the Indian Ocean. Why was this? Costas Synolakis, a professor of civil engineering at USC, answered the question in the *Wall Street Journal* days after the disaster. "The angry questions that hundreds of thousands of family members of victims are asking are 'what happened?'—and 'why did no one warn us before the tsunami hit?'"

The Pacific Tsunami Warning Center (PTWC) had issued a tsunami bulletin and had concluded that there was no danger for the Pacific nations in its jurisdiction. Why didn't it extend its warning to South and Southeast Asia? It is perhaps clear in hindsight that an Indian Ocean tsunami warning center should have been in place, or that the Indian Ocean nations should have requested coverage from the PTWC. Clearly, the hazard had been grossly underestimated. To give governments the benefit of the doubt, the last transoceanic tsunami that hit the region occurred on April 27, 1883, and this was caused by Krakatoa's eruption (36,000 people killed). Other large earthquakes along the Sumatra trench had not caused major tsunamis, or, if they had, they had not been reported as devastating. Floods occur nearly every year in that area of the world, as do hurricanes. Natural hazards that are less frequent tend to be ignored. No nation can be ready for every eventuality—as 9/11 painfully demonstrated—at least before a major disaster identifies the risk.

The painful reality of 9/11 was that the pattern of signals of the terrorists at work before the event was subtle and obscure. As the authors of the 9/11 Report made clear, "insight for the future is thus not easy to apply in practice. It is hardest to mount a major effort while a problem still seems minor. Once the danger has fully materialized, evident to all, mobilizing action is easier—but it then may be too late."

To return to the subject of the two 9/11 terrorists who had provided American officials with early signals—Khalid al-Midhar and Nawaf al-Hazmi—one can see in hindsight the dilemma faced by our intelligence agencies. The CIA, along with local intelligence officials in Kuala Lumpur, picked up the trail of al-Midhar and al-Hazmi in January 2000 at a meeting in that city, but the CIA did not watchlist al-Midhar or notify the FBI when it learned al-Midhar possessed a valid US visa. Al-Midhar and al-Hazmi flew from Kuala Lumpur to Bangkok and then to Los Angeles on January 15. The problem for intelligence officials was that simply tracking two Arabs who might be part of "an operational cadre" was not a pressing task. There were no earlier signals to connect these two to a larger plot. Unlike Captain Smith of the *Titanic*, who had sufficient information about icebergs in his path, intelligence officials dealing with the early movements of the 9/11 terrorists were three or four steps behind even shaping the outlines of a plot. As the commissioners reported:

"Even if watchlisting had prevented or at least alerted U.S. officials to the entry of Hazmi and Midhar, we do not think it is likely that watchlisting, by itself, would have prevented the 9/11 attacks. Al Qaeda adapted to the failure of some of its operatives to gain entry into the United States. None of these future hijackers was a pilot. Alternatively, had they been permitted entry and surveilled, some larger results might have been possible had the FBI been patient. These are difficult what-ifs. The intelligence community might have judged that the risks of conducting such a prolonged intelligence operation were too high—potential terrorists might have been lost track of, for example. The pre-9/11 FBI might not have been judged capable of conducting such an operation. But surely the intelligence community would have preferred to have the chance to make these choices."

Unfortunately, our intelligence agencies possessed neither the imagination nor the resources to make those choices. Officers on board the *Titanic* had enough information prior to the disaster to avoid it. Intelligence officials in the 9/11 case would have been shooting in the dark had they even been prepared to fire. The key would have been to identify the relevance of al-Hazmi and al-Midhar to a potential plot. As Cofer Black recalled, the movements of al-Hazmi and al-Midhar were "considered interesting, but not heavy water yet." Even in hindsight, the commissioners sympathized with the failure of the acting officials. "One can see how hard it is for the intelligence community to assemble enough of the puzzle pieces gathered by different agencies to make some sense of them and then develop a fully informed joint plan. Accomplishing all this is especially difficult in a transnational case. We sympathize with the working level officers, drowning in information and trying to decide what is important or what needs to be done when no particular action has been requested of them."

Comment (from page 62): In reviewing aspects of the *Challenger* disaster, one wonders why the space shuttle fuel tanks were built with O-rings in the first place. James R. Chiles, in his illuminating book, *Inviting Disaster: Lessons From The Edge of Technology*, provides an answer: "Because the manufacturer was in Utah, and because a fully assembled booster was too big to move across land in a single piece, each rocket motor traveled to Kennedy Space Center by railroad, broken into four main cylindrical segments. Workers at Kennedy stacked the segments together vertically and topped the stack with the nose cone, making up a full length booster. Thiokol called the connection between each segment the 'field-joint' because the work was done in the field, meaning outside the factory. Each booster needed three field joints along the fuel-containing length. To visualize how a field joint works, imagine trying to string short pipes together into a high-pressure pipeline in such a way that you could disassemble and reassemble the whole pipeline every few months. You couldn't weld the pipes; you'd have to use some kind of mechanical joint with removable fasteners…To keep the flame at the core of the booster where it belonged, the field joints had heat-resistant putty to close off the gap between the fuel castings, and two rubber O-rings fitted into the rim-and-slot arrangement as a final seal."

Comment (from page 65): A curious footnote about Thomas Andrews was brought to light by Steven Biel in his masterful book, *Down With The Old Canoe: A Cultural History of the Titanic Disaster.* "One of the stories told in all the versions of *A Night To Remember* involved a young Philadelphia couple, Mr. and Mrs. Lucien Smith. In the TV broadcast the Smiths enjoy the consummate modern marriage, based on loving companionship and consumption. The gender theme is introduced early, when the ship's designer, Thomas Andrews, complains to his steward, Alfred, that nobody is retiring to the ladies' writing room after dinner. Alfred observes that 'the ladies of the twentieth century are not as retiring as formerly'—in other words, that they are now attractive and entertaining companions to their husbands rather than quiet exemplars of duty and sacrifice."

Comment (from page 79): A postscript on the *Titanic* story. Members of the team investigating the crash of the space shuttle *Columbia* released their report in late August 2003 and found conclusively that a piece of insulating foam caused the tragedy. In an article in the November 2003 edition of *The Atlantic*, William Langewiesche reviews how the *Columbia* disaster unfolded, particularly the aspects of the NASA culture which enabled it. Many of the elements of that disaster mirror what happened to the *Titanic* and to the previous space shuttle failure, *Challenger.*

About a minute-and-a-half after lift-off, as the *Columbia* was accelerating past 1,500 miles-per-hour, a piece of foam used to insulate the external fuel tank—the big, orange tank forming the center of the overall vehicle at lift-off—came loose and collided with the shuttle's left wing at about 545 mph. That piece of foam weighed just under two pounds and was about nineteen inches long by eleven inches wide. NASA officials monitoring the flight were not overly concerned. Foam strikes, after all, were a relatively normal occurrence even though, technically, foam was not supposed to shed from the external tank. Usually, the falling foam was the size of popcorn and, therefore, too small to cause more than superficial dents in the thermal protection tiles.

The culture, or groupthink, of NASA began to view foam strikes as an "in-family" problem. Because these foam strikes were familiar and non-threatening, their concerns were tossed into the mundane world of garden-variety concerns of the NASA managers. Here's where the similarities to the *Challenger* disaster arise. In the *Challenger* case, O-rings around the external fuel tanks began, by degrees, to allow hot gases to penetrate outwards. This was particularly a problem in cold weather. However, as each space shuttle flight returned safely, NASA officials grew less and less concerned with the O-ring problem and, as one commentator put it, began to "normalize the deviance." So, too, Captain Smith of the *Titanic* had made many trips across the Atlantic, had seen many icebergs in time to slow down his ships. Therefore, in his mind, and in the minds of his officers, icebergs were of relatively little danger. Such was the case with foam strikes in the *Columbia* disaster. Here is the telling commentary from Langewiesche's article:

"The shuttle managers acted as if they thought the frequency of the foam strikes had somehow reduced the danger that the impacts posed. The point was not that the managers really believed this but that after more than a hundred successful flights they had come blithely to accept the risk. . . Like the astronauts and NASA itself, the managers were trapped by a circular space policy thirty years in the making, and they had no choice but to strive to meet the timelines directly ahead. As a result, after the most recent *Atlantis* launch, in October of 2002, during which a chunk of foam from a particularly troublesome part of the external tank, known as the bipod ramp, had dented one of the solid rocket boosters, shuttle managers formally decided during the post-flight review not to classify the incident as an 'in-flight anomaly.' This was the first time that a serious bipod ramp incident had escaped such a classification. The decision allowed the following two launches to proceed on schedule. The second of those launches was the *Columbia's* on January 16, 2003."

The flight of *Columbia* met all the thresholds for failure. Even though the problem had been identified, those foam strikes—like O-rings or icebergs—had never been serious enough to change the thinking of the managers in charge. Unfortunately, once that one foam strike crossed the threshold of danger, those in charge could not reasonably envision altering the course of the deviance.

Videos of the *Columbia* foam strike make it clear that the offending material had come from the area of the bipod ramp, that this time the foam was larger than ever before, that the impact had occurred later in the climb when the speed was greater, and that the left wing had been hit, but exactly where was unclear. The astronauts, happily now in orbit, were unaware of any problem. Responsibility for dealing with the problem lay with the Mission Management Team, or MMT, whose purpose was to make decisions about the problems and unscripted events that inevitably arose during any flight. The MMT was headed by Ron Dittemore, who was traveling at the time. Therefore, the reins of power rested in the hands of his chief lieutenant, Linda Ham, an aggressive, intimidating woman, taken to wearing low-cut clothing, and with the breezy, business-like manner of a career woman on the upward climb in a culture dominated by men.

According to *The Atlantic* article, Ham's style got the best of her on the sixth day of the mission when she uttered a few words too many. This came at the end of a report given by a mid-ranking engineer named Don McCormack, who summarized the progress of a hastily-assembled engineering group formed solely to analyze the foam strike. McCormack reported that little was yet resolved, but that some work was being done to explore the options should the analysis conclude that the *Columbia* had been seriously damaged. "After a brief exchange, Ham cut him short, saying: 'And I'm really. . .I don't think there is much we can do, so it's

146

not really a factor during the flight, since there is not much we can do about it.' . . . This was a dangerous business, and she knew it all too well. But like her boss, Ron Dittemore, with whom she discussed the *Columbia* foam strike several times, she was so immersed in the closed world of shuttle management that she simply did not elevate the event—this 'in-family' thing—to the level of concerns requiring action. She was intellectually arrogant, perhaps, and as a manager she failed abysmally. But neither she nor the others of her rank had the slightest suspicion that the *Columbia* might actually go down."

In hindsight, those of us who investigate these disasters have the luxury of focusing on the one element that caused the chain of failures which led to the disaster—in this case, the foam strike. But those NASA managers, or the officers on board the *Titanic*, had many, many other things to worry about. A foam strike or the proximity of an iceberg were relatively unimportant in relation to other elements of the mission or journey. In this case, the deviation (a foam strike during launch) had been identified, but since all the shuttle missions had been safely completed in spite of such foam strikes, this particular foam strike was given no more importance than any of the others and, therefore, no more urgency. In addition to this, and unlike the *Titanic*, the culture of NASA lends itself to decentralized problem-solving. As the independent head of the investigating team said:

"They claim that the culture in Houston is a 'badge-less' society, meaning it doesn't matter what you have on your badge—you're concerned about shuttle safety together. Well, that's all nice, but the truth is that it does matter what badge you're wearing. Look, if you really do have an organization that has free communication and open doors and all that kind of stuff, it takes a special kind of management to make it work. And we just don't see that management here. Oh, they say all the right things. 'We have open doors and e-mails, and anybody who sees a problem can raise his hand, blow a whistle, and stop the whole process.' But then when you look at how it really works, it's an incestuous, hierarchical system, with invisible rankings and a very strict informal chain of command. They all know that. So even though they've got all the trappings of communications, you don't actually find communication. It's very complex. But if a person brings an issue up, what caste he's in makes all the difference. Now, again, NASA will deny this, but if you talk to people, if you really listen to people, all the time you hear, 'Well, I was afraid to speak up.' Boy, it comes across loud and clear. You listen to the meetings: 'Anybody got anything to say?' There are thirty people in the room and slam! There's nothing. We have plenty of witness statements saying, 'If I had spoken up, it would have been at the cost of my job.' And if you're in the engineering department, you're a nobody."

So, here's the scenario. The shuttle takes off. A piece of foam breaks off from the surface of the external fuel tank and strikes the shuttle, but NASA managers don't know the precise location of that strike. And, in the meantime, there are other things to worry about, other issues. The team, or teams, assigned to worry about this particular issue get bogged down in bureaucracy and the fear within the NASA culture of finger-pointing or whistle-blowing. In the meantime, the

Columbia's crew were orbiting the gorgeous orb of earth, blissfully unaware of what amounts to a gaping ten inch hole in the leading edge of the shuttle's left wing, which, upon re-entry into the earth's atmosphere, would fill with hot, pulverizing gas that could break through a dam. A communication to the two pilots aboard the space shuttle concluded: "There is one item that I would like to make you aware of for the upcoming PAO event. . . This item is not even worth mentioning other than wanting to make sure that you are not surprised by it in a question from a reporter." And, after describing the strike from the bipod ramp foam, the communication continued: "Experts have reviewed the high speed photography and there is no concern for wing or tile damage. We have seen this same phenomenon on several other flights and there is absolutely no concern for entry. That is all for now. It's a pleasure working with you every day."

Was Linda Ham correct that, even if NASA had accurately identified the lethal nature of this problem, there was "not much" they could do about it? Not exactly. First, NASA could have bought the orbiting *Challenger* another month of time. By then the space shuttle *Atlantis*, scheduled for a March 1 lift-off, could have been made ready for an early February departure. "If all had proceeded perfectly, there would have been a five-day window in which to blast off, join up with the *Columbia*, and transfer the stranded astronauts one by one to safety, by means of tethered spacewalks. Such a rescue would not have been easy, and it would have involved the possibility of another fatal foam strike and the loss of two shuttles instead of one, but in the risk-versus-risk world of space flight, veterans like Mike Bloomfield would immediately have volunteered, and NASA would have bet the farm."

Bet the farm, indeed! This space walk rescue would have been a national spectacle. Our attention, briefly, would have been diverted from any saber-rattling in the Middle East. And an unprecedented media blitz would have made the Apollo 13 drama look like child's play. Short of this rescue, the other alternative would have been a more desperate measure—"a jury rigged repair performed by the *Columbia* astronauts themselves. It would have required two spacewalkers to fill the hole with a combination of heavy tools and metal scraps scavenged from the crew compartment, and to supplement that mass with an ice bag shaped to the wing's leading edge. In theory, if much of the payload had been jettisoned, and luck was with the crew, such a repair might perhaps have endured a modified re-entry and allowed the astronauts to bail out at the standard 30,000 feet."

But the problem, of course, is that in spite of all the successful shuttle flights, or all the successful transatlantic crossings, there always seems to be some remote failure lurking out there—whether it be rubber O-rings gradually degenerating or a looming blue iceberg or insulating foam breaking away in flight. Given the enormously complex nature of space shuttle flight, under the auspices of such danger, it is a wonder there haven't been more catastrophes than just two.

A Note on Notes

While I researched these three men and each of their episodes, I was, of course, inspired by the work of other authors. In the case of Custer, it was Evan S. Connell's book, *Son of The Morning Star*; in the case of the *Titanic*, it was Walter Lord's contribution—his twins—*A Night To Remember* and *The Night Lives On*. For Edward Grey, I found that Barbara Tuchman's *The Guns of August* and Robert K. Massie's *Dreadnought* were both remarkable renditions of how the Great War came about.

A Postscript to the Introduction

Re: Afghanistan and the Russian-Ukraine War.

1 A full report on the Afghan withdrawal issued just before the July 4th, 2023, holiday said the Biden Administration officials in Washington were to blame for failing to decide which Afghans should be eligible for evacuation and for issuing constantly changing guidelines. Left behind by the hasty 2021 exit were most Afghan allies who had applied for a visa program aimed to save those at risk of Taliban retribution for cooperating with American forces. Instead, tens of thousands of unvetted Afghans were able to make it through the Kabul Airport to be evacuated. The confusion of constantly changing the guidelines for evacuation and the failure to heed critical facts on the ground contributed to the deaths of 13 US service members and over a hundred Afghans at the airport perimeter. The report said that both the Biden and Trump Administrations shared responsibility for the failures. "During both administrations there was insufficient senior-level consideration of worst-case scenarios and how quickly those might follow."

2. Former US President Bill Clinton has said he feels a "personal stake" in Ukraine's war with Russia because of his role in persuading Kiev to surrender their nuclear weapons under the Budapest Agreement. "None of them believe that Russia would have pulled this stunt if Ukraine still had their weapons," he said. Did the 2014 takeover of Crimea help pave the way for the Spring 2022 invasion of Ukraine? Undoubtedly. At the time, America could have relied on the Budapest Memorandum to gather a coalition of willing participants to erect a naval quarantine of Russia in the Black Sea. Instead, much like the US Government's policy towards native Americans, we got wavering, moving targets, no well-reasoned, consistent foreign policy. As one commentator noted: "All of this, however, ducks the one big question asked of any modern President's foreign policy: What exactly do you guys stand for? What, when you've left the building, will the United States represent? After more than five years of Obama foreign policy, what we've got is a huge fuzzball of good intentions. It doesn't stand for anything--not a strategy, not a set of identifiable ideas, no real doctrine and not much to show for whatever it is." (Daniel Henninger, Wall Street Journal, March 2014)

AN ASIDE ON CUSTER

Edward S. Godfrey's comments on the Battle of the Little Bighorn appear in Part One. For many years after its first appearance in the *Century Magazine* for January 1892, General Godfrey's article titled "Custer's Last Battle" was generally accepted as the one authoritative account available to the public. Below, we reprint that portion of the article that covers Custer's movements and preparations leading up to the battle.

Preparations
On our arrival at the mouth of the Rosebud, Generals Terry, Gibbon, and Custer had a conference on board the steamer Far West. It was decided that the 7th Cavalry, under General Custer, should follow the trail discovered by Reno. "Officers' call" was sounded in the 7th Cavalry camp as soon as the conference had concluded. Upon assembling, General Custer gave us our orders. We were to transport, on our pack-mules, fifteen days' rations of hard bread, coffee and sugar; twelve days' rations of bacon, and fifty rounds of carbine ammunition per man. Each man was supplied with 100 rounds of carbine and 24 rounds of pistol ammunition to be carried on his person and in his saddle bags. Each man was to carry on his horse twelve pounds of oats.

The pack-mules sent out with Reno's command were badly used up, and promised seriously to embarrass the expedition. General Custer recommended that some extra forage be carried on the pack-mules. In endeavoring to carry out this recommendation some troop commanders (Captain Moylan and myself) foresaw the difficulties, and told the General that some of the mules would certainly break down, especially if the extra forage was packed. He replied in an unusually emphatic manner. "Well, gentlemen, you may carry what supplies you please; you will be held responsible for your companies. The extra forage was only a suggestion, but this fact bear in mind, we will follow the trail for fifteen days unless we catch them before that time expires, no matter how far it may take us from our base of supplies; we may not see the supply steamer again"; and, turning as he was about to enter his tent, he added: "You had better carry along an extra supply of salt; we may have to live on horse meat before we get through." He was taken at his word, and an extra supply of salt was carried. "Battalion" and "wing" organizations were broken up, and troop commanders were responsible only to General Custer. Of course, as soon as it was determined that we were to go out, nearly every one took time to write letters home, but I doubt very much if there were many of a cheerful nature. Some officers made their wills; others gave verbal instructions as to the disposition of personal property and distribution of mementos; they seemed to have a presentiment of their fate.

The Hostiles
There were a number of Sioux Indians who never went to an agency except to visit friends and relatives and to barter. They camped in and roamed about the buffalo

country. Their camp was the rendezvous for the agency Indians when they went out for their annual hunts for meats and robes. They were known as the "Hostiles," and comprised representatives from all the different tribes of the Sioux nation. Many of them were renegade outlaws from the agencies. In their visits to the agencies they were usually arrogant and fomenters of discord. Depredations had been made upon the commerce to the Black Hills, and a number of lives taken by them or by others, for which they were blamed. The authorities at Washington had determined to compel these Indians to reside at the agencies—hence the Sioux War.

Major James McLaughlin, United States Indian Agent, stationed at the Devil's Lake Agency, Dakota, from 1870 to 1881, and at Standing Rock Agency, Dakota, from 1881 to 1895, and to the present time Inspector in the Bureau of Indian Affairs, has made it a point to get estimates of the number of Indians at the hostile camp at the time of the battle. In his opinion, and all who know him will accept it with confidence, about one-third of the whole Sioux nation, including the northern Cheyennes and Arapahoes, were present at the battle; he estimates the number present as between twelve and fifteen thousand; that one out of four is a low estimate in determining the number of warriors present; every male over fourteen years of age may be considered a warrior in a general fight, such as was the battle of the Little Big Horn; also, considering the extra hazards of the hunt and expected battle, fewer squaws would accompany the recruits from the agencies. The minimum strength of their fighting men may then be put down as between twenty-five hundred and three thousand. Information was dispatched from General Sheridan that from the agencies about 1800 lodges had set out to join the hostile camp; but that Information did not reach General Terry until several days after the battle. The principal warriors chiefs of the hostile Indians were Gall, Crow King and Black Moon, Huncpapa Sioux; Spotted Eagle, Sans-Arc Sioux; Hump of the Minneconjous; and White Bull and Little Horse of the Cheyennes. To these belong the chief honors of conducting the battle; however, Gall, Crow King and Crazy Horse were the ruling spirits.

Sitting Bull
Sitting Bull, a Huncpapa Sioux Indian, was the chief of the hostile camp; he had about sixty lodges of followers on whom he could at all times depend. He was the host of the Hostiles, and as such received and entertained their visitors. These visitors gave him many presents, and he was thus enabled to make many presents, in return. All visitors paid tribute to him, so he gave liberally to the most influential, the chiefs, i.e. he "put it where it would do the most good." In this way he became known as the chief of the hostile camp, and the camp was generally known as "Sitting Bull's camp" or "outfit." Sitting Bull was a heavy set, muscular man, about five feet eight inches in stature, and at the time of the battle of the Little Big Horn was forty-two years of age. He was the autocrat of the camp—chiefly because he was the host. In council his views had great weight, because he was known as a great medicine man. He was a chief, but not a warrior chief. In the war councils he had a voice and vote the same as any other chief. A short time previous to the

battle he had "made medicine," had predicted that the soldiers would attack them and that the soldiers would all be killed. He took no active part in the battle, but, as was his custom in time of danger, remained in the village "making medicine." Personally, he was regarded by the Agency Indians as a great coward and a very great liar, "a man with a big head and a little heart."

The War Chief Gall

Chief Gall was born about 1840, of Huncpapa parents. Until Sitting Bull's surrender, 1881, Gall never lived at the agencies, but was sometimes a guest. When 25 years old he was noted for his bravery and daring. He was so subtle, crafty and daring, that in 1886, the military authorities offered a reward for his body, dead or alive; an outrage had been committed, which for daring and craftiness, it was thought no other Indian was gifted. However, he was innocent. Gall knew of the price laid on his carcass and kept away from the military. At Fort Berthold, while visiting friends at the Agency, his visit was made known to the commanding officer at Fort Stevenson, a few miles away. A detachment was sent to the tepee where he was visiting, to arrest him. On their entrance Gall dropped on his belly and pushed himself backward under the tepee. A soldier on the outside bayoneted him through the body and held him till he fainted. The soldiers supposed him to be dead, and so reported to their commander. They were sent back with transportation to get the body. Great was their astonishment to find that Gall had recovered consciousness and crawled away. The men searched faithfully the woods in which Gall had concealed himself, but he was not discovered. Gall then got back to his people and vowed vengeance. He had it in many a foray and numbers of battles. He lurked about the military posts and pounced on luckless promenaders, even at the very gates of the stockade that enclosed the barracks and quarters. He raided settlements and attacked Black Hill stages and freighters. He it was who followed the "Bozeman Expedition" about 1874, for days, when they were searching for gold, compelling them at all times to be in readiness for battle. One of their entrenchments may yet be seen on the divide between the Rosebud and Little Big Horn at the head of Thompson Creek.

In 1872 he led his braves in a raiding attack on the 2nd Cavalry at "Baker's Battlefield" on the Yellowstone, which by reason of its surprise, came near proving a disaster, as Indians rarely made night attacks. August 4th, 1873, General Custer had gone into bivouac on the north bank of the Yellowstone, just above Fort Keogh, waiting for the main command under General Stanley. The two troops had unsaddled and were resting in the supposed security afforded by the absence of fresh "Indian signs," while Gall made his dispositions for the attack. His warriors crawled through woods, down ravines and under the river bank to within 300 yards when an alarm called to arms and a lively battle was kept up until the arrival of troops from the main command which had heard and seen the firing from the mesa several miles away. A week later Gall made an attack on the 7th Cavalry at the head of "Pease Bottom," a few miles below the mouth of the Big Horn. In this fight Gall, dressed in brilliant scarlet and war bonnet, rode back and forth in front of the firing line, the target of hundreds of shots, but escaped unharmed. He was the Great War Chief of all the Sioux at "Custer's Last Battle." In 1877 he went with Sitting Bull to Canada, and in 1881 surrendered at Poplar Creek, Montana. The band was taken into Standing Rock Agency, 1882, by steamboat. The boat was met by a great throng of people; the military, settlers and employees and Indians of that Agency were at the landing. When the boat was tied up, Gall, in full war paint and regalia ostentatiously walked down the gang plank, halted and surveyed the surroundings. His old mother ran to him and tried to gain his notice; she got on her knees, clasped him about his legs took hold of and kissed his hand; she moaned and cried. Ignoring her caresses, he stalked dramatically aboard the boat. Later Gall became reconciled to agency life and was a good Indian; wise and conservative, he supported the Agent, Major James McLaughlin, in all his efforts for the good of the people. In the grand councils of all the Chiefs of the Sioux nation, he was the most influential and stood up for what he considered the just rights of his people. He died at Oak Creek, near Standing Rock Agency, in 1895. His features were massive, and in facial appearance was compared to the great expounder, Webster; to Henry Ward Beecher and to Bishop Newman. He was a man of great natural ability, force of character and possessed great common sense.

Instructions
General Custer's written instructions were as follows:
Camp at Mouth of Rosebud River, Montana Territory, June 22nd, 1876. Lieut.-Col. Custer, 7th Cavalry.

Colonel:
The Brigadier-General Commanding directs that, as soon as your regiment can be made ready for the march, you will proceed up the Rosebud in pursuit of the Indians whose trail was discovered by Major Reno a few days since. It is, of course, impossible to give any definite instructions in regard to this movement, and were it not impossible to do so, the Department Commander places too much confidence in your zeal, energy, and ability to wish to impose upon you precise orders which might hamper your action when nearly in contact with the enemy. He will, however, indicate to you his own views of what your action should be, and he desires that you should conform to them unless you shall see sufficient reason for departing from them. He thinks that you should proceed up the Rosebud until you ascertain definitely the direction in which the trail above spoken of leads. Should it be found (as it appears almost certain that it will be found) to turn toward the Little Horn, he thinks that you should still proceed southward, perhaps as far as the headwaters of the Tongue, and then turn toward the Little Horn, feeling constantly, however, to your left, so as to preclude the possibility of the escape of the Indians to the south or southeast by passing around your left flank. The column of Colonel Gibbon is now in motion for the mouth of the Big Horn. As soon as it reaches that point it will cross the Yellowstone and move up at least as far as the forks of the Big and Little Horns. Of course its future movements must be controlled by circumstances as they arise, but it is hoped that the Indians, if upon the Little Horn, may be so nearly inclosed by the two columns that their

escape will be impossible.

The Department Commander desires that on your way up the Rosebud you should thoroughly examine the upper part of Tullock's Creek, and that you should endeavor to send a scout through to Colonel Gibbon's column, with information of the result of your examination. The lower part of the creek will be examined by a detachment from Colonel Gibbon's command. The supply steamer will be pushed up the Big Horn as far as the forks if the river is found to be navigable for that distance, and the Department Commander, who will accompany the column of Colonel Gibbon, desires you to report to him there not later than the expiration of the time for which your troops are rationed, unless in the meantime you receive further orders.

Very respectfully,
Your obedient servant,
E. W. Smith, Captain, 18th Infantry,
Acting Assistant Adjutant-General.

These instructions are explicit, and fixed the location of the Indians very accurately. It has been assumed by some writers that General Terry's command would be at the mouth of the Little Big Horn on June 26th, and that General Custer knew of that—also by some that the two commands were to come together about that date at that place. General Terry's instructions do not say when his command would reach that point, and according to the instructions, General Custer was not necessarily expected there before the 5th or 6th of July, being rationed for fifteen days.

The March Up The Rosebud
At twelve o'clock, noon, on the 22nd of June, the "Forward" was sounded, and the regiment marched out of camp in column of fours, each troop followed by its pack-mules. Generals Terry, Gibbon and Custer stationed themselves near our line of march and reviewed the regiment. General Terry had a pleasant word for each officer as he returned the salute. Our pack-trains proved troublesome at the start, as the cargoes began falling off before we got out of camp, and during all that day the mules straggled badly. After that day, however, they were placed under the charge of Lieutenant Mathey, who was directed to report at the end of each day's march the order of merit of the efficiency of the troop packers. Doubtless, General Custer had some ulterior design in this. It is quite probable that if he had had occasion to detach troops requiring rapid marching, he would have selected those troops whose packers had the best records. At all events the efficiency was much increased, and after we struck the Indian trail the pack-trains kept well closed. We went into camp about 4 p.m., having marched twelve miles. About sunset "officers' call" was sounded, and we assembled at General Custer's bivouac and squatted in groups about the General's bed. It was not a cheerful assemblage; everybody seemed to be in a serious mood, and the little conversation carried on, before all had arrived, was in undertones. When all had assembled, the General

154

said that until further orders, trumpet calls would not be sounded except in an emergency; the marches would begin at 5 a.m. sharp; the troop commanders were all experienced officers, and knew well enough what to do, and when to do what was necessary for their troops; there were two things that would be regulated from his headquarters, i.e. when to move out of and when to go into camp. All other details, such as reveille, stables, watering, halting, grazing, etc., on the march would be left to the judgment and discretion of the troop commanders; they were to keep within supporting distance of each other, not to get ahead of the scouts, or very far to the rear of the column. He took particular pains to impress upon the officers his reliance upon their judgment, discretion, and loyalty. He thought, judging from the number of lodge-fires reported by Reno, that we might meet at least a thousand warriors; there might be enough young men from the agencies, visiting their hostile friends, to make a total of fifteen hundred. He had consulted the reports of the Commissioner of Indian Affairs and the officials while in Washington as to the probable number of "Hostiles" (those who had persistently refused to live or enroll themselves at the Indian agencies), and he was confident, if any reliance was to be placed upon these reports, that there would not be an opposing force of more than fifteen hundred. General Terry had offered him the additional force of the battalion of the 2nd Cavalry, but he had declined it because he felt sure that the 7th Cavalry could whip any force that would be able to combine against him, that if the regiment could not, no other regiment in the service could; if they could whip the regiment, they would be able to defeat a much larger force, or, in other words, the reinforcement of this battalion could not save us from defeat. With the regiment acting alone, there would be harmony, but another organization would be sure to cause jealousy or friction. He had declined the offer of the Gatling guns for the reason that they might hamper our movements or march at a critical moment, because of the inferior horses and of the difficult nature of the country through which we would march. The marches would be from twenty-five to thirty miles a day. Troop officers were cautioned to husband their rations and the strength of their mules and horses, as we might be out for a great deal longer time than that for which we were rationed, as he intended to follow trail until we could get the Indians, even if it took us to the Indian agencies on the Missouri River or in Nebraska. All officers were requested to make to him any suggestions they thought fit.

This "talk" of his, as we called it, was considered at the time as something extraordinary for General Custer, for it was not his habit to unbosom himself to his officers. In it he showed concessions and a reliance on others; there was an indefinable something that was *not* Custer. His manner and tone, usually brusque and aggressive, or somewhat curt, was on this occasion conciliating and subdued. There was something akin to an appeal, as if depressed, that made a deep impression on all present. We compared watches to get the official time, and separated to attend to our various duties. Lieutenants McIntosh, Wallace (killed at the Battle of Wounded Knee, December 29, 1890), and myself walked to our bivouac, for some distance in silence, when Wallace remarked: "Godfrey, I believe General Custer is going to be killed." "Why? Wallace," I replied, "what makes you think so?" "Because," said he, "I have never heard Custer talk in that way before."

I went to my troop and gave orders what time the "silent" reveille should be and as to other details for the morning preparations; also the following directions in the case of a night attack: the stable guard, packers, and cooks were to go out at once to the horses and mules to quiet and guard things the other men were to go out at once to a designated rendezvous and await orders; no man should fire a shot until he received orders from an officer to do so. When they retired for the night they should put their arms and equipments where they could get them without leaving their beds. I then went through the herd to satisfy myself as to the security of the animals. During the performance of this duty I came to the bivouac of the Indian scouts. "Mitch" Bouyer, the half-breed interpreter, "Bloody Knife," the chief of the Ree scouts; "Half-Yellow-Face," the chief of the Crow scouts, and others were having a "talk." I observed them for a few minutes, when Bouyer turned toward me, apparently at the suggestion of "Half-Yellow-Face" and said; "Have you ever fought against these Sioux?" "Yes," I replied. Then he asked, "Well, how many do you expect to find?" I answered, "It is said we may find between one thousand and fifteen hundred." "Well, do you think we can whip that many?" "Oh, yes, I guess so." After he had interpreted our conversation, he said to me with a good deal of emphasis, "Well, I can tell you we are going to have a damned big fight." At five o'clock sharp, on the morning of the 23rd, General Custer mounted and started up the Rosebud, followed by two sergeants, one carrying the regimental standard, and the other his personal or headquarters flag, and the same kind of flag he used while commanding his cavalry division during the Civil War. This was the signal for the command to mount and take up the march. Eight miles out we came to the first Indian camping places. It certainly indicated a large village and numerous population. There were a great many "wickiups" (bushes stuck in the ground with the tops drawn together, over which they placed canvas or blankets). These we supposed at the time were for the dogs, but subsequent events developed the fact that they were temporary shelters of the transients from the agencies. During the day we passed through three of these camping places and made halts at each one. Everybody was busy studying the age of the pony droppings and tracks and lodge trails, and endeavoring to determine the number of lodges. These points were all-absorbing topics of conversation. We went into camp about five o'clock, having marched about thirty-three miles.

June 24th we passed a great many camping places, all appearing to be of nearly the same strength. One would naturally suppose these were the successive camping-places of the same village, when, in fact, they were the continuous camps of the several bands. The fact that they appeared to be of nearly the same age, that is, having been made at the same time, did not impress us then. We passed through one much larger than any of the others. The grass for a considerable distance around it had been cropped close, indicating that large herds had been grazed there. The frame of a large "Sun-Dance" lodge was standing, and in it we found the scalp of a white man. It was whilst here that the Indians from the agencies had joined the Hostiles' camp. The command halted here and the "officers' call" was sounded. Upon assembling we were informed that our Crow scouts, who had been

156

very active and efficient, had discovered fresh signs, the tracks of three or four ponies and one Indian on foot. At this point a stiff southerly breeze was blowing; as we were about to separate, the General's headquarters' flag was blown down, falling toward our rear. Being near the flag I picked it up and stuck the staff in the ground, but it again fell to the rear. I then bored the staff into the ground where it would have the support of a sagebrush. This circumstance made no impression on me at the time, but after the battle, an officer, Lieutenant Wallace, asked me if I remembered the incident. He had observed, and regarded the fact of its falling to the rear as a bad omen, and felt sure we would suffer a defeat.

The march during the day was tedious. We had many long halts, so as not to get ahead of the scouts, who seemed to be doing their work thoroughly, giving special attention to the right, toward Tullock's Creek, the valley of which was in general view from the divide. Once or twice signal smokes were reported in that direction, but investigations did not confirm the reports. The weather was dry and had been for some time, consequently the trail was very dusty. The troops were required to march on separate trails, so that the dust clouds would not rise so high. The valley was heavily marked with lodge-pole trails and pony tracks, showing that immense herds of ponies had been driven over it. About sundown we went into camp under the cover of a bluff, so as to hide the command as much as possible. We had marched about twenty-eight miles. The fires were ordered to be put out as soon as supper was over, and we were to be in readiness to march again at 11:30 p.m.

Lieutenant Hare and myself lay down about 9:30 to take a nap. When comfortably fixed, we heard some one say, "He's over there by that tree." As that described my location pretty well, I called out to know what was wanted, and the reply came: "The General's compliments, and he wants to see all the officers at headquarters immediately." So we gave up our much-needed rest and groped our way through horse herds, over sleeping men and through thickets of bushes trying to find headquarters. No one could tell us, and as all fires and lights were out we could not keep our bearings. We finally espied a solitary candle-light, toward which we traveled and found most of the officers assembled at the General's bivouac. The General said that the trail led over the divide to the Little Big Horn; the march would be taken up at once, as he was anxious to get as near the divide as possible before daylight, where the command would be concealed during the day, and give ample time for the country to be studied, to locate the village, and to make plans for the attack on the 26th. We then returned to our troops, except Lieutenant Hare, who was put on duty with the scouts. Because of the dust, it was impossible to see any distance and the rattle of equipments and clattering of the horses' feet made it difficult to hear distinctly beyond our immediate surroundings. We could not see the trail and we could only follow it by keeping in the dust cloud. The night was very calm, but occasionally a slight breeze would waft the cloud and disconcert our bearings; then we were obliged to halt to catch a sound from those in advance, sometimes whistling or hallooing, and getting a response we could start forward again. Finally, troopers were put ahead, away from the noise of our column, and where they could hear the noise of those in front. A little after 2 a.m., June 25th, the command was halted to await further tidings from the scouts; we had marched about ten miles. Part of the command unsaddled to rest the horses. After daylight some coffee was made, but it was impossible to drink it; the water was so alkaline that the horses refused to drink it.

Some time before eight o'clock, General Custer rode bareback to the several troops and gave orders to be ready to march at eight o'clock, and gave information that scouts had discovered the locality of the Indian villages or camps in the valley of the Little Big Horn, about twelve or fifteen miles beyond the divide. Just before setting out on the march, I went to where General Custer's bivouac was. The General, "Bloody Knife," and several Ree scouts and a half-breed interpreter were squatted in a circle, having a "talk" after the Indian fashion. The general wore a serious expression and was apparently abstracted. The scouts were doing the talking, and seemed nervous and disturbed. Finally "Bloody Knife" made a remark that recalled the General from his reverie, and he asked in his usual quick, brusque manner, "What's that he says?" The interpreter replied: "He says we'll find enough Sioux to keep up fighting two or three days." The General smiled and remarked, "I guess we'll get through with them in one day."

We started promptly at eight o'clock and marched uninterruptedly until 10:30 a.m. when we halted in a ravine and were ordered to preserve quiet, keep concealed, and not do anything that would be likely to reveal our presence to the enemy. We had marched about ten miles.

It is a rare occurrence in Indian warfare that gives a commander the opportunity to reconnoiter the enemy's position in daylight. This is particularly true if the Indians have a knowledge of the presence of troops in the country. When following an Indian trail the "signs" indicate the length of time elapsed since the presence of the Indians. When the "signs" indicate a "hot trail" i.e. near approach, the commander judges his distance and by a forced march, usually in the night time, tries to reach the Indian village at night and make his disposition for a surprise attack at daylight. At all events his attack must be made with celerity, and generally without other knowledge of the numbers of the opposing force than that discovered or conjectured while following the trail. The disposition for the attack may be said to be "made in the dark," and successful surprise to depend upon luck. If the advance to attack be made in daylight it is next to impossible that a near approach can be made without discovery. In all our previous experiences, when the immediate presence of the troops was once known to them, the warriors swarmed to the attack, and resorted to all kinds of ruses to mislead the troops, to delay the advance toward their camp or village while the squaws and children secured what personal effects they could, drove off the pony herd, and by flight put themselves beyond danger, and then scattering, made successful pursuit next to impossible. In civilized warfare the hostile forces may confront each other for hours, days or weeks, and the battle may be conducted with a tolerable knowledge of the numbers, positions, etc. of each other. A full knowledge of the immediate presence of the enemy does not imply immediate attack. In Indian warfare the rule is "touch and go." In fact, the firebrand nature of Indian warfare is not generally understood. In mediating upon the preliminaries of an Indian battle, old soldiers who have participated only in the battles of "civilized" war are apt to draw upon their own experiences for compassion, when there is no comparison.

Troops Discovered

It was well known to the Indians that the troops were in the field, and a battle was fully expected by them; but the close proximity of our column was not known to them until the morning of the day of the battle. Several young men had left the hostile camp on that morning to go to one of the agencies in Nebraska. They saw the dust made by the column of troops; some of their number returned to the village and gave warning that the troops were coming, so the attack was not a surprise. For two or three days their camp had been pitched on the site where they were attacked. The place was not selected with the view to making that the battle-field of the campaign, but, whoever was in the van on their march thought it a good place to camp, put up his tepee, and the others as they arrived followed his example. (This was Gall's explanation.) It is customary among the Indians to camp by bands. The bands usually camp some distance apart, and Indians of the number then together would occupy a territory of several miles along the river valley, and not necessarily within supporting distance of each other. But in view of the possible fulfillment of Sitting Bull's prophecy the village had massed.

The Little Big Horn River, or the "Greasy Grass" as it is known to the Indians, is a rapid, tortuous mountain stream from twenty to forty yards wide, with pebbled bottom, but abrupt, soft banks. The water at the ordinary stage is from two or five feet in depth, depending upon the width of the channel. The general direction of its course is northeasterly down to the Little Big Horn battle-fields, where it trends northwesterly to its confluence with the Big Horn River. The other topographical features of the country which concern us in this narrative may be briefly described as followed: Between the Little Big Horn and Big Horn Rivers is a plateau of undulating prairie; between the Little Big Horn and the Rosebud are the Little Chetish or Wolf Mountains. By this it must not be misunderstood as a rocky upheaval chain or spur of mountains, but it is a rough, broken country of considerable elevation, of high precipitous hills and deep, narrow gulches. The command had followed the trail up a branch of the Rosebud to within, say, a mile of the summit of these mountains, which form the "divide." Not many miles to our right was the divide between the Little Big Horn and Tulloch's Fork. The creek that drained the watershed to our right and front is now variously called "Sun-Dance," Benteen's, or Reno's Creek. The trail, very tortuous, and sometimes dangerous, followed down the bed and valley of the south branch of this creek, which at that time was dry for the greater part of its length. It was from the divide between the Little Big Horn and the Rosebud that the scouts had discovered the smoke rising above the village, and the pony herds grazing in the valley of the Little Big Horn, somewhere about twelve or fifteen miles away. It was to their point of view that General Custer had gone while the column was halted in the ravine. It was impossible for him to discover more of the enemy than had already been reported by the scouts. In consequence of the high bluffs which screened the village, it was not possible in following the trail to discover more. Nor was there a point of observation near the trail from which further discoveries could be made until the battle was at hand.

Our officers had generally collected in groups and discussed the situation. Some sought solitude and sleep, or meditation. The Ree scouts, who had not been very active for the past day or two, were together and their "medicine man" was anointing them and invoking the Great Spirit to protect them from the Sioux. They seemed to have become satisfied that we were going to find more Sioux than we could well take care of. Captain Yates' troop had lost one of its packs of hard bread during the night march from our last halting place on the 24th. He had sent a detail back on the trail to recover it. Captain Keogh came to where a group of officers were and said this detail had returned and Sergeant Curtis, in charge, reported that when near the pack they discovered an Indian opening one of the boxes of hard bread with his tomahawk, and that as soon as the Indian saw the soldiers he galloped away to the hills, out of range and then moved along leisurely. This information was taken to the General at once by his brother, Captain Tom Custer. The General came back and had "officers' call" sounded. He recounted Captain Keogh's report, and also said that the scouts had seen several Indians move along the ridge overlooking the valley through which we had marched, as if observing our movements; he thought the Indians must have seen the dust made by the command. At all events, our presence had been discovered and further concealment was unnecessary; that we would move at once to attack the village; that he had not intended to make the attack until the morning, the 26th, but our discovery made it imperative to act at once, as delay would allow the village to scatter and escape. Troop commanders were ordered to make a detail of one non-commissioned officer and six men to accompany the pack; to inspect their troops and report as soon as they were ready to march; that the troops would take their places in column of march in order in which reports of readiness were received; the last one to report would escort the pack-train.

The above material was reprinted in The Custer Myth: A Source Book of Custeriana, *written and compiled by Colonel W.A. Graham, published by Bonanza Books, New York, NY, 1953.*

AN ASIDE ON THE TITANIC

Below is the testimony of Bruce Ismay before the 1912 US Senate panel investigating the disaster. This material came from *The Titanic Disaster Hearings: The Official Transcripts of the 1912 Senate Investigations* edited by Tom Kuntz, published by Pocket Books, New York, NY, 1998.

The First Day
Friday, April 19, 1912
The Waldorf-Astoria Hotel, New York

The opening session was called to order by Senator William Alden Smith at 10:30 in the morning in the hotel's crystal-chandeliered East Room—a Gilded Age setting if ever there was one—now crammed to standing-room-only capacity with reporters and curious spectators, many from New York's upper class.

Seated next to Senator Smith, on one side of a conference table, were Senator Francis G. Newlands, Democrat of Nevada, the Senate subcommittee's vice chairman; and George Uhler, inspector general of the Commerce Department's steamboat inspection service, an advisor to Smith.

Across from them at the table was the first witness, J. Bruce Ismay, head of White Star, the *Titanic*'s cruise line, also president of the International Mercantile Marine Co., White Star's American parent, financed by J.P. Morgan, Jr. (who had canceled his trip on the *Titanic*). Seated with Ismay were his American vice president, Philip A. S. Franklin; the *Titanic*'s senior surviving officer, Second Officer Charles Lightoller; IMM attorneys; and bodyguards detailed to protect Ismay, who in the four days since the disaster had been villainized in the American press for not staying with his ship.

Witness: J. Bruce Ismay, 49
Managing director of the White Star Line and first-class passenger, from Liverpool, England

Key testimony: Ismay, who later would be summoned back before the panel, elicited broad skepticism in his initial appearance with evasive statements like, "More than that I do not know." He denied that the *Titanic* had been pushed to its maximum speed, though Senator Smith would ultimately conclude that Ismay's presence on the ship was a factor encouraging Capt. Edward J. Smith to go faster. Asked how he managed to get away in a lifeboat when many passengers, including women and children, were unable to, Ismay said there were no more women or children in the vicinity of the boat that he had been helping to load and the boat still had room, so he got in. He said that as the *Titanic* sank, he did not look back because he was "pulling away" with his back to the ship: "I did not wish to see her go down." Asked to explain why he wouldn't be facing the wreck if he were rowing away from it, Ismay said that on his lifeboat the oars had to be pushed.

WAS: Will you kindly tell the committee the circumstances surrounding your voyage, and, as succinctly as possible, beginning with your going aboard the vessel at Liverpool, your place on the ship on the voyage, together with any circumstances you feel would be helpful to us in this inquiry?

JBI: In the first place, I would like to express my sincere grief at this deplorable catastrophe.

I understand that you gentlemen have been appointed as a committee of the Senate to inquire into the circumstances. So far as we are concerned, we welcome it. We court the fullest inquiry. We have nothing to conceal; nothing to hide. The ship was built in Belfast. She was the latest thing in the art of shipbuilding; absolutely no money was spared in her construction. She was not built by contract. She was simply built on commission.

She left Belfast, as far as I remember am not absolutely clear about these dates—I think it was on the 1st of April.

She underwent her trials, which were entirely satisfactory. She then proceeded to Southampton; arriving there on Wednesday.

WAS: Will you describe the trials she went through?

JBI: I was not present.

She arrived at Southampton on Wednesday, the 3rd, I think, and sailed on Wednesday, the 10th. She left Southampton at 12 o'clock. She arrived in Cherbourg that evening, having run over at 68 revolutions [propeller revolutions per minute].

We left Cherbourg and proceeded to Queenstown. We arrived there, I think, about midday on Thursday.

We ran from Cherbourg to Queenstown at 70 revolutions.

After embarking the mails and passengers, we proceeded at 70 revolutions. I am not absolutely clear what the first day's run was, whether it was 464 miles or 484 miles.

The second day the number of revolutions was increased. I think the number of revolutions on the second day was about 72. I think we ran on the second day 519 miles.

The third day the revolutions were increased to 75, and I think we ran 546 or 549 miles.

The weather during this time was absolutely fine, with the exception, I think, of about 10 minutes' fog one evening.

The accident took place on Sunday night. What the exact time was I do not know. I was in bed myself, asleep, when the accident happened.

The ship sank, I am told, at 2:20.

That, sir, I think is all I can tell you.

I understand it has been stated that the ship was going at full speed. The ship never had been at full speed. The full speed of the ship is 78 revolutions. She works up to 80. So far as I am aware, she never exceeded 75 revolutions. She had not all her boilers on. None of the single-ended boilers were on.

It was our intention, if we had fine weather on Monday afternoon or Tuesday, to drive the ship at full speed. That owing to the unfortunate catastrophe, never eventuated.

WAS: Will you describe what you did after the impact or collision?

JBI: I presume the impact awakened me. I lay in bed for a moment or two afterwards, not realizing, probably, what had happened. Eventually I got up and walked along the passageway and met one of the stewards, and said, "What has happened?" He said, "I do not know, sir."

I then went back into my room, put my coat on, and went up on the bridge, where I found Capt. Smith. I asked him what had happened, and he said, "We have struck ice." I said, "Do you think the ship is seriously damaged?" He said, "I am afraid she is."

I then went down below, I think it was, where I met Mr. Bell, the chief engineer, who was in the main companionway. I asked if he thought the ship was seriously damaged, and he said he thought she was, but was quite satisfied the pumps would keep her afloat.

I think I went back onto the bridge. I heard the order given to get the boats out. I walked along to the starboard side of the ship, where I met one of the officers. I told him to get the boats out.

WAS: What officer?

JBI: That I could not remember, sir.

I assisted, as best I could, getting the boats out and putting the women and children into the boats.

I stood upon that deck practically until I left the ship in the starboard collapsible boat, which is the last boat to leave the ship, so far as I know. More than that I do not know.

WAS: Did the captain remain on the bridge?

JBI: That I could not tell you, sir.

WAS: Did you leave him on the bridge?

JBI: Yes, sir.

WAS: His first statement to you was that he felt she was seriously damaged?

JBI: Yes, sir.

WAS: And the next statement of the chief engineer was what?

JBI: To the same effect.

WAS: To the same effect?

JBI: Yes.

WAS: But that he hoped the pumps might keep her afloat?

JBI: Yes.

WAS: Did you have any talk with any officer other than the captain or the chief engineer and the steward that you met?

JBI: Not that I remember.

WAS: Did the officers seem to know the serious character of this collision?

JBI: That I could not tell, sir, because I had no conversation with them.

WAS: Did any officer say to you that it evidently was not serious?

JBI: No, sir.

WAS: All the officers with whom you talked expressed the same fear, saying that it was serious?

JBI: I did not speak to any of them, sir.

WAS: Except the captain?

JBI: Except the captain and the chief engineer. I have already stated that I had spoken to them; but no other officer that I remember.

WAS: You went to the bridge immediately after you had returned to your room?

JBI: After I had put on my coat I went up to the bridge.

WAS: And you found the captain there?

JBI: The captain was there.

WAS: In what part of the ship were your quarters?

JBI: My quarters were on B deck, just aft on the main companionway.

WAS: I wish you would describe just where that was.

JBI: The sun deck is the upper deck of all. Then we have what we call the A deck, which is the next deck, and then the B deck.

WAS: The second passenger deck?

JBI: We carry very few passengers on the A deck. I think we have a diagram here that will show you these decks. Here it is, and there is the room I was occupying [indicating on diagram].

WAS: What is the number of that room?

JBI: B-52 is the room I had.

WAS: You had the suite?

JBI: I had the suite; I was sleeping in that room [indicating on diagram], as a matter of fact.

WAS: Do you know whether there were any passengers on that deck?

JBI: I have no idea sir.

WAS: You say that the trip was a voluntary trip on your part?

JBI: Absolutely.

WAS: For the purpose of viewing this ship in action, or did you have some business in New York?

JBI: I had no business to bring me to New York at all. I simply came in the natural course of events, as one is apt to, in the case of a new ship, to see how she works, and with the idea of seeing how we could improve on her for the next ship which we are building.

WAS: Were there any other executive officers of the company aboard?

JBI: None.

WAS: Was the inspector or builder on board?

JBI: There was a representative of the builders on board.

WAS: Who was he?

JBI: Mr. Thomas Andrews.

WAS: In what capacity was he?

JBI: I do not quite follow you.

WAS: What was the occasion for his coming to make this trial trip?

JBI: As a representative of the builders, to see that everything was working satisfactorily, and also to see how he could improve the next ship.

WAS: Was he a man of large experience?

JBI: Yes.

WAS: Had he had part in the construction of this ship himself?

JBI: Yes.

WAS: Was he among the survivors?

JBI: Unfortunately, no.

WAS: How old a man was he?

JBI: It is difficult to judge a man's age, as you know, but I should think he was perhaps 42 or 43 years of age. He may have been less. I really could not say.

WAS: Then, you were the only executive officer aboard representing your company, aside from the ship's customary complement of officers?

JBI: Yes, sir.

WAS: Did you have occasion to consult with the captain about the movement of the ship?

JBI: Never.

WAS: Did he consult you about it?

JBI: Never. Perhaps I am wrong in saying that. I should like to say this: I do not know that it was quite a matter of consulting him about it, or of his consulting me about it, but what we had arranged to do was that we would not attempt to arrive in New York at the lightship before 5 o'clock on Wednesday morning.

WAS: That was the understanding?

JBI: Yes. But that was arranged before we left Queenstown.

WAS: Was it supposed that you could reach New York at that time without putting the ship to its full running capacity?

JBI: Oh, yes, sir. There was nothing to be gained by arriving at New York any earlier than that.

WAS: You spoke of the revolutions on the early part of the voyage.

JBI: Yes, sir.

WAS: Those were increased as the distance was increased?

JBI: The *Titanic* being a new ship, we were gradually working her up. When you bring out a new ship you naturally do not start running her at full speed until you get everything working smoothly and satisfactorily down below.

WAS: Did I understand you to say that she exceeded 70 revolutions?

JBI: Yes, sir; she was going 75 revolutions on Tuesday.

WAS: On Tuesday?

JBI: No; I am wrong—on Saturday. I am mixed up as to the days.

WAS: The day before the accident?

JBI: The day before the accident. That, of course, is nothing near her full speed.

WAS: During the voyage, do you know, of your own knowledge, of your proximity to icebergs?

JBI: Did I know that we were near icebergs?

WAS: Yes.

JBI: No, sir; I did not. I know ice had been reported.

WAS: Ice had been reported?

JBI: Yes.

WAS: Did you personally see any icebergs, or any large volume of ice?

JBI: No; not until after the accident.

WAS: Not until after the wreck?

JBI: I had never seen an iceberg in my life before.

WAS: You never saw one before.

JBI: No, sir.

WAS: Had you ever been on this so-called northern route before?

JBI: We were on the southern route, sir.

WAS: On this Newfoundland route?

JBI: We were on the long southern route; not on the northern route.

WAS: You were not on the extreme northern route?

JBI: We were on the extreme southern route for the west-bound ships.

WAS: What was the longitude and latitude of this ship? Do you know?

JBI: That I could not tell you; I am not a sailor.

WAS: Were you cognizant of your proximity to icebergs at all on Saturday?

JBI: On Saturday? No sir.

WAS: Do you know anything about a wireless message from the [German liner] *Amerika* to the *Titanic*?

JBI: No, sir.

WAS: Saying that the *Amerika* had encountered ice in that latitude?

JBI: No, sir.

WAS: Were you aware of the proximity of icebergs on Sunday?

JBI: On Sunday? No; I did not know on Sunday. I knew that we would be in the ice region that night sometime.

WAS: That you would be or were?

JBI: That we would be in the ice region on Sunday night.

WAS: Did you have any consultation with the captain regarding the matter?

JBI: Absolutely none.

WAS: Or with any other officer of the ship?

JBI: With no officer at all, sir. I was absolutely out of my province. I am not a navigator. I was simply a passenger on board the ship.

WAS: Do you know anything about the working of the wireless service on this ship?

JBI: In what way? We had wireless on the ship.

WAS: Had you taken any unusual precaution to have a reserve power of this wireless?

JBI: I believe there was, but I have no knowledge of that myself.

WAS: Do you know how long the wireless continued to operate after the blow or collision?

JBI: No, sir; I do not.

WAS: Did you, at any time, see the operator of the wireless?

JBI: I did not.

WAS: Did you attempt to send any messages yourself?

JBI: I did not.

WAS: Were you outside on the deck, or on any deck, when the order was given to lower the lifeboats.

JBI: I heard Capt. Smith give the order when I was on the bridge.

WAS: You heard the captain give the order?

JBI: Yes, sir.
WAS: Will you tell us what he said.
JBI: It is very difficult for me to remember exactly what was said, sir.
WAS: As nearly as you can.
JBI: I know I heard him give the order to lower the boats. I thing that is all he said. I think he simply turned around and gave the order.
WAS: Was there anything else said, as to how they should be manned or occupied?
JBI: No, sir; not that I heard. As soon as I heard him give the order to lower the boats, I left the bridge.
WAS: You left the bridge?
JBI: Yes.
WAS: Did you see any of the boats lowered?
JBI: Yes, sir.
WAS: How many?
JBI: Certainly three.
WAS: Will you tell us, if you can, how they were lowered?
JBI: They were swung out, people were put into the boats from the deck, and then they were simply lowered away down to the water.
WAS: Were these lifeboats on various decks?
JBI: They were all on one deck.
WAS: On what deck?
JBI: On the sun deck; the deck above this [indicating on diagram]. I do not think it is shown on this plan.
WAS: That is, the second deck above yours.
JBI: On this deck here, on the big plan [indicating].
WAS: On the sun deck?
JBI: Yes; on what we call the sun deck or the boat deck.
WAS: They were on the boat deck, which would be the upper deck of all?
JBI: The upper deck of all, yes.
WAS: Was there any order or supervision exercised by the officers of the ship in loading these lifeboats?
JBI: Yes, sir.
WAS: I wish you would tell just what that was.
JBI: That I could not say. I could only speak from what I saw for myself.
WAS: That is all I wish you to do.
JBI: The boats that were lowered where I was were in charge of the officer and were filled and lowered away.
WAS: They first put men into the boats for the purpose of controlling them?
JBI: We put in some of the ship's people.
WAS: Some of the ship's people?
JBI: Yes.
WAS: How many?
JBI: That I could not say.
WAS: About how many?
JBI: I could not say.

167

WAS: About three or four?

JBI: The officer who was there will be able to give you that information, sir. My own statement would be simply guesswork. His statement would be reliable.

WAS: In the boat in which you left the ship how many men were on board?

JBI: Four.

WAS: Besides yourself?

JBI: I thought you meant the crew.

WAS: I did mean the crew.

JBI: There were four of the crew.

WAS: What position did these men occupy?

JBI: I do not know, sir.

WAS: Were any of them officers?

JBI: No.

WAS: Or seamen?

JBI: I believe one was a quartermaster.

WAS: One was a quartermaster?

JBI: I believe so, but I do not know.

WAS: You saw three of the boats lowered yourself?

JBI: Yes.

WAS: And three of them loaded?

JBI: Yes.

WAS: As they were loaded, was any order given as to how they should be loaded?

JBI: No.

WAS: How did it happen that the women were first put aboard these lifeboats?

JBI: The natural order would be women and children first.

WAS: Was that the order?

JBI: Oh, yes.

WAS: That was followed?

JBI: As far as practicable.

WAS: So far as you observed?

JBI: So far as I observed.

WAS: And were all the women and children accommodated in these lifeboats?

JBI: I could not tell you, sir.

WAS: How many passengers were in the lifeboat in which you left the ship?

JBI: I should think about 45.

WAS: Forty-five?

JBI: That is my recollection.

WAS: Was that its full capacity?

JBI: Practically.

WAS: How about the other two boats?

JBI: The other three, I should think, were fairly loaded up.

WAS: The three besides the one you were in?

JBI: Yes.

WAS: They were fairly well filled?

JBI: Yes.

WAS: Was there any struggle or jostling?

JBI: I saw none.

WAS: Or any attempt by men to get into the boats?

JBI: I saw none.

WAS: Were these women passengers designated as they went into the lifeboat?

JBI: No, sir.

WAS: Those that were nearest the lifeboat were taken in?

JBI: We simply picked the women out and put them in the boat as fast as we could.

WAS: You picked them from among the throng?

JBI: We took the first ones that were there and put them in the lifeboats. I was there myself and put a lot in.

WAS: You helped put some of them in yourself?

JBI: I put a great many in.

WAS: Were children shown the same consideration?

JBI: Absolutely.

WAS: Did you see any lifeboat without its complement of oarsmen?

JBI: I did not.

WAS: Did you see the first lifeboat lowered?

JBI: I could not answer, sir. I was the first lifeboat lowered on the starboard side. What was going on the port side I have no knowledge of.

WAS: It has been intimated, Mr. Ismay, that the first lifeboat did not contain the necessary number of men to man it.

JBI: As to that I have no knowledge, sir.

WAS: And that women were obliged to row the boat.

JBI: That is the second lifeboat, Senator.

WAS: The second lifeboat; and that women were obliged to row that boat from 10:30 o'clock at night until 7:30 o'clock the next morning.

JBI: The accident did not take place until 11.

WAS: Well, from after 11:30 o'clock at night until between 6 and 7 o'clock the next morning.

JBI: Of that I have no knowledge.

WAS: Until the *Carpathia* overtook them. You have no knowledge of that?

JBI: Absolutely none, sir.

WAS: So far as your observation went, would you say that was not so?

JBI: I would not say either yes or no; but I did not see it.

WAS: When you first went on the deck, you were only partially clothed?

JBI: That is all, sir.

WAS: And, as I understand, you went as far as to encounter an officer or steward?

JBI: Yes, sir.

WAS: And then returned?

JBI: That is right.

WAS: How long were you on the ship after the collision occurred?

JBI: That is a very difficult question to answer, sir. Practically until the time— almost until she sank.

WAS: How long did it take to lower and load a lifeboat?

JBI: I could not answer that.

WAS: Can you approximate it?

JBI: It is not possible for me to judge the time. I could not answer that.

WAS: Were you on the *Titanic* an hour after the collision?

JBI: Oh, yes.

WAS: How much longer?

JBI: I should think it was an hour and a quarter.

WAS: An hour and a quarter?

JBI: I should think that was it; perhaps longer.

WAS: Did you, during this time, see any of the passengers that you knew?

JBI: I really do not remember; I saw a great many passengers, but I do not think I paid much very attention to who they were. I do not remember recognizing any of them.

WAS: Did you know [the Canadian railroad magnate] Charles M. Hayes?

JBI: Yes, sir.

WAS: Did you know of the presence of other Americans and Canadians of prominence?

JBI: No, sir; I knew Mr. Hayes was on board the ship.

WAS: You knew he was on the ship?

JBI: Yes, I have known him for some years.

WAS: But did you not see him after the accident occurred?

JBI: I never saw him after the accident; no.

WAS: And he is unaccounted for?

JBI: Yes, sir.

WAS: He was not among the saved?

JBI: No, sir.

WAS: What were the circumstances, Mr. Ismay, of your departure from the ship?

JBI: In what way?

WAS: Did the last boat that you went on leave the ship from some point near where you were?

JBI: I was immediately opposite the lifeboat when she left.

WAS: Immediately opposite?

JBI: Yes.

WAS: What were the circumstances of your departure from the ship? I ask merely that—

JBI: The boat was there. There was a certain number of men in the boat, and the officer called out asking if there were any more women, and there was no response, and there were no passengers left on the deck.

WAS: There were no passengers on the deck?

JBI: No, sir; and as the boat was in the act of being lowered away, I got into it.

WAS: At the time the *Titanic* was sinking?

JBI: She was sinking.

WAS: Where did this ship collide? Was it a side blow?

JBI: I have no knowledge, myself. I can only state what I have been told, that she hit the iceberg somewhere between the breakwater and the bridge.

WAS: State that again.

JBI: Between the breakwater and the bridge.

WAS: On the starboard side?

JBI: Yes.

WAS: Did you see any of the men passengers on that ship with life preservers on?

JBI: Nearly all passengers had life preservers on.

WAS: All that you saw?

JBI: All that I saw had life preservers on.

WAS: All of them that you saw?

JBI: Yes; as far as I can remember.

WAS: Naturally, you would remember that if you saw it? When you entered the lifeboat yourself, you say there were no passengers on that part of the ship?

JBI: None.

WAS: Did you, at any time, see any struggle among the men to get into these boats?

JBI: No.

WAS: Was there any attempt, as this boat was being lowered past the other decks, to have you take on more passengers?

JBI: None, sir. There were no passengers there to take on.

WAS: Before you boarded the lifeboat, did you see any of the passengers or crew with life-saving apparatus on them in the sea?

JBI: No, sir.

WAS: What course was taken by the lifeboat in which you were after leaving the ship?

JBI: We saw a light some distance off to which we attempted to pull and which we thought was a ship.

WAS: Can you give the direction of it?

JBI: I could not give that.

WAS: But you saw a light.

JBI: Yes, sir.

WAS: And you attempted to pull this boat toward it?

JBI: Yes, sir.

WAS: How long were you in the open sea in this lifeboat?

JBI: I should think about four hours.

WAS: Were there any other lifeboats in that vicinity?

JBI: Yes.

WAS: How many?

JBI: That I could not answer. I know there was one, because we hailed her. She had a light, and we hailed her, but got no answer from her.

WAS: You got no answer?

JBI: No, sir.

WAS: Did you see any rafts on the *Titanic* that could have been utilized?

JBI: I believe not.

WAS: Were all the lifeboats of one type?

JBI: No; there were four that are called collapsible boats.

WAS: What were the others?

JBI: Ordinary wooden boats.

WAS: How many were there?

JBI: I think there were 20 altogether.

WAS: Including both designs?

JBI: Yes. Sixteen wooden boats and four collapsible boats, I think. I am not absolutely certain.

WAS: When you reached the *Carpathia*, was your lifeboat taken aboard the *Carpathia*?

JBI: That I do not know.

WAS: Did you see any other lifeboats taken aboard the *Carpathia*?

JBI: I did not.

WAS: What was the method of getting you aboard the *Carpathia*?

JBI: We simply walked up a Jacob's ladder.

WAS: What was the condition of the sea at that time?

JBI: There was a little ripple on it, nothing more.

WAS: Do you know whether all the lifeboats that left the *Titanic* were accounted for?

JBI: I believe so. I do not know that of my own knowledge.

WAS: I think it has been suggested that two of them were engulfed.

JBI: Of that I know nothing.

WAS: You would know if that were true, would you not?

JBI: I have had no consultation with anybody since the accident with the exception of one officer.

WAS: Who was that?

JBI: Mr. Lightoller. I have spoken to no member of the crew or anybody since in regard to the accident.

WAS: What was Mr. Lightoller's position?

JBI: He was the second officer of the *Titanic*.

WAS: How many officers of the ship's crew were saved?

JBI: I am told four.

WAS: Can you give their names?

JBI: I can not.

WAS: Or their occupation?

JBI: I could not. The only one I know is Mr. Lightoller, who was the second officer.

WAS: I understand they are here.

JBI: I believe so; I do not know.

WAS: Mr. Ismay, what can you say about the sinking and disappearance of the ship? Can you describe the manner in which she went down?

JBI: I did not see her go down.

WAS: You did not see her go down?

JBI: No, sir.

WAS: How far were you from the ship?

JBI: I do not know how far we were away. I was sitting with my back to the ship. I was rowing all the time I was in the boat. We were pulling away.

WAS: You were rowing?

JBI: Yes; I did not wish to see her go down.

WAS: You did not care to see her go down?

JBI: No. I am glad I did not.

WAS: When you last saw her, were there indications that she had broken in two?

JBI: No, sir.

WAS: When did you last see her?

JBI: I really could not say. It might have been 10 minutes after we left her. It is impossible for me to give any judgment of the time. I could not do it.

WAS: Was there much apparent confusion on board when you saw her last?

JBI: I did not look to see, sir. My back was turned to her. I looked around once only, to see her red light—her green light, rather.

WAS: You never saw the captain again after you left him on the bridge?

JBI: No, sir.

WAS: Did you have any message from him?

JBI: Nothing.

WAS: Do you know how many wireless operators there were on board the ship?

JBI: I do not; but I presume there were two. There is always one on watch.

WAS: Do you know whether they survived?

JBI: I am told one of them did, but I do not know whether it is true or not. I really have not asked.

WAS: Were any of this crew enlisted men in the English Navy?

JBI: I do not know, sir. The ship's articles will show that.

WAS: Can you tell us anything about the inspection, and the certificate that was made and issued before sailing?

JBI: The ship receives a board of trade passenger certificate; otherwise she would not be allowed to carry passengers.

WAS: Do you know whether that was done?

JBI: You could not sail your ship without it; you could not get your clearance.

WAS: Do you know whether this ship was equipped with its full complement of lifeboats?

JBI: If she had not been, she could not have sailed. She would not have received her passenger certificate; therefore she must have been fully equipped.

WAS: Do you know whether these lifeboats were the lifeboats that were planned for the *Titanic*?

JBI: I do not understand what you mean, sir. I do not think lifeboats are ever built for the ship. Lifeboats are built to have a certain cubic capacity.

WAS: I understand that; but I mean whether these lifeboats were completed for the ship coincident with the completion of the ship, or whether the lifeboats, or any of them, were borrowed from the other ships of the White Star Line?

JBI: They certainly would not be borrowed from any other ship.

WAS: Do you recollect whether the lifeboat in which you left the ship was marked with the name *Titanic* on the boat or on the oars?

JBI: I have no idea. I presume oars would be marked. I do not know whether the boat was marked or not. She was a collapsible boat.

WAS: Can you recollect whether that was so?

JBI: I did not look to see whether the oars were marked. It would be a natural precaution to take?

WAS: Mr. Ismay, do you know about the boiler construction of the *Titanic*?

JBI: No, sir; I do not.

May I suggest, gentlemen, if you wish any information in regard to the construction of the ship, in any manner, shape, or form, that I shall be only too pleased to arrange for one of the Harland & Wolff's people to come here and give you all the information you require; the plans and everything.

WAS: We are much obliged to you.

There has been some suggestion by passengers who left the ship in lifeboats, that an explosion took place after this collision. Have you any knowledge on that point?

JBI: Absolutely none.

WAS: Do you think you would have known about that if it had occurred?

JBI: Yes; I should. Do you mean to say before the ship went down?

WAS: Yes.

JBI: Absolutely.

WAS: Mr. Ismay, do you know anything about the action of the amidship turbine; the number of revolutions?

JBI: No.

MR. UHLER: The reciprocating engines, you say, were going at 75 or 72 revolutions at one time?

JBI: Yes.

MR. UHLER: Have you any knowledge as to how many revolutions the amidship turbine was making?

JBI: No, sir. Those are all technical questions which can be answered by others, if you desire.

SENATOR NEWLANDS: What speed would 75 revolutions indicate?

JBI: I should think about 21 knots.

SENATOR NEWLANDS: What is that in miles?

JBI: It is in the ratio of 11 to 13; about 26 miles, I think.

SENATOR NEWLANDS: Mr. Ismay, did you have anything to do with the selection of the men who accompanied you in the last boat?

JBI: No, sir.

SENATOR NEWLANDS: How were they designated?

JBI: I presume by the officer who was in charge of the boat.

SENATOR NEWLANDS: Who was that?

JBI: Mr. Weyl [Chief Officer Henry Wilde].

SENATOR NEWLANDS: And he was what officer?

JBI: Chief officer.

SENATOR NEWLANDS: Was that done by lot or by selection?

JBI: I think these men were allotted certain posts.

SENATOR NEWLANDS: Indiscriminately?

JBI: No; I fancy at the time they had what they called, I think, the boat's crew list. That is all arranged beforehand.

WAS: Can you describe those rafts?

JBI: There were none on board the ship.

WAS: Did you see any rafts actually in service?

JBI: No, sir.

WAS: Is it customary for the White Star Line to carry rafts?

JBI: I believe in the olden days we carried rafts.

WAS: Recently that has not been done?

JBI: Not in recent ships; no, sir.

WAS: Why?

JBI: I presume because they are not considered suitable.

WAS: Do you know what water capacity there was on that ship?

JBI: I do not, sir.

WAS: I mean, when she was stove in, how many compartments could be flooded with safety?

JBI: I beg your pardon, sir. I misunderstood your question. The ship was especially constructed to float with two compartments full of water.

WAS: She was constructed to float with two compartments full of water?

JBI: The ship was specially constructed so that she would float with any two compartments full of water. I think I am right in saying that there are very few ships—perhaps I had better not say that, but I will continue, now that I have begun it—I believe there are very few ships today of which the same can be said.

When we built the *Titanic* we had that especially in mind. If this ship had hit the iceberg stem on, in all human probability she would have been here to-day.

WAS: If she had hit the iceberg head on, in all probability she would be here now?

JBI: I say in all human probability that ship would have been afloat to-day.

SENATOR NEWLANDS: How did the ship strike the iceberg?

JBI: From information I have received, I think she struck the iceberg a glancing blow between the end of the forecastle and the captain's bridge, just aft of the foremast, sir.

WAS: I understood you to say a little while ago that you were rowing, with your back to the ship. If you were rowing and going away from the ship, you would naturally be facing the ship, would you not?

JBI: No; in these boats some row facing the bow of the boat and some facing the stern. I was seated with my back to the man who was steering, so that I was facing away from the ship.

WAS: You have stated that the ship was specially constructed so that she could float with two compartments filled with water?

JBI: Yes.

WAS: Is it your idea, then, that there were no two compartments left entire?

JBI: That I could not answer, sir. I am convinced that more than two compartments were filled. As I tried to explain to you last night, I think the ship's bilge was ripped open.

SENATOR NEWLANDS: The ship had 16 compartments?

JBI: I could not answer that, sir.

SENATOR NEWLANDS: Approximately?

JBI: Approximately. That information is absolutely at your disposal. Our shipbuilders will give it to you accurately.

SENATOR NEWLANDS: She was so built that if any two of these compartments should be filled with water she would still float?

JBI: Yes, sir; if any two of the largest compartments were filled with water she would still float.

WAS: Mr. Ismay, what time did you dine on Sunday evening?

JBI: At 7:30.

WAS: With whom?

JBI: With the doctor.

WAS: Did the captain dine with you?

JBI: He did not, sir.

WAS: When you went to the bridge after this collision was there any ice on the decks?

JBI: I saw no ice at all, and no icebergs at all until daylight Monday morning.

WAS: Do you know whether any people were injured or killed from ice that came on the decks?

JBI: I do not, sir. I heard ice had been found on the decks, but it is only hearsay.

WAS: I think I asked you, but in case it appears that I have not, I will ask you again: Were all of the women and children saved?

JBI: I am afraid not, sir.

WAS: What proportion were saved?

JBI: I have no idea. I have not asked. Since the accident I have made few inquiries of any sort.

WAS: Did any of the collapsible boats sink, to your knowledge, after leaving the ship?

JBI: No, sir.

SENATOR NEWLANDS: What was the full equipment of lifeboats for a ship of this size?

JBI: I could not tell you that, sir. That is covered by the board of trade regulations. She may have exceeded the board of trade regulation, for all I know. I could not answer that question. Anyhow, she had sufficient boats to obtain her passenger certificate, and therefore she must have been fully boated, according to the requirements of the English Board of Trade, which I understand are accepted by this country. Is not that so, General?

MR. UHLER: Yes.

WAS: Mr. Ismay, did you in any manner attempt to influence or interfere with the wireless communication between the *Carpathia* and other stations?

JBI: No, sir. I think the captain of the *Carpathia* is here, and he will probably tell you that I was never out of my room from the time I got on board the *Carpathia* until the ship docked here last night. I never moved out of the room.

WAS: How were you dressed? Were you completely dressed when you went into the lifeboat?

JBI: I had a suit of pajamas on, a pair of slippers, a suit of clothes, and an overcoat.

WAS: How many men, officers and crew, were there on this boat?

JBI: There were no officers.

WAS: I mean the officers of the ship.

JBI: How many officers were there on the ship?

WAS: Yes, and how many in the crew?

JBI: I think there were seven officers on the ship.

WAS: And how many in the crew?

JBI: I do not know the full number of the crew. There were seven officers—or nine officers; there are always three officers on watch.

WAS: And how many men were in the lifeboat with you?

JBI: Oh, I could not tell. I suppose nine or ten.

WAS: Do you know who they were?

JBI: I do not. Mr. [William] Carter, a passenger [a wealthy Philadelphian], was one. I do not know who the others were; third-class passengers, I think. In fact, all the people on the boat, as far as I could see, were third-class passengers.

WAS: Did they all survive, and were they all taken aboard the *Carpathia*?

JBI: They all survived, yes.

An Aside on World War I

Below are some of the documents exchanged between several of the principals involved in the heated diplomacy leading up to the outbreak of World War One. This material was taken from the book, *July 1914: The Outbreak of the First World War: Selected Documents*, edited by Imanuel Geiss, published by W.W. Norton, New York, NY, 1967.

Bethmann Hollweg to Lichnowsky
Telegram
> Berlin, 3 August 1914
> D. 10.25 p.m.

Please state to Sir Edward Grey that if we should take the step of violating Belgian neutrality, we would do so compelled by the duty of self-preservation. We found ourselves in position of military constraint. While France had also before that time made strong military preparations and while we had up until then confined ourselves in a military way to only the most urgent measures of military preparation for self-defence, the unfortunate Russian mobilization had suddenly exposed us to the danger of being swallowed up by the floods from east and west. The preliminaries of the French mobilisation had demonstrated that mobilisation is fated to bring war in its train. Then, wedged in between east and west, we had to make use of every means to save ourselves. It is not by any means a case of intentional violation of international law, but the act of a man fighting for his life. I had devoted all my efforts as Imperial Chancellor toward gradually bringing about, in partnership with England, a state of affairs which would make the madness of self-destruction on the part of Europe's civilised nations impossible. Russia, by treacherously playing with fire, has brought these intentions to naught. Say that I firmly hope that England, by her attitude in this world crisis, will lay a foundation on which, after it has come to an end, we may bring to realisation all that Russia's policy has for present destroyed.

Jagow to Below
Telegram
> Berlin, 3 August 1914
> R. 10.35 p.m.

Your Excellency will inform the Belgian Government tomorrow, Tuesday, 4 August, at six a.m., that, to our regret, we shall be forced by its attitude of refusal toward our well-meant proposals, to put into execution the measures of self-protection against the French menace which we have already described as unavoidably necessary, even if we have to do it by force of arms.

Paul Cambon to Viviani
Telegram
London, 3 August 1914

D. 11.52 a.m.

R. 2.30 p.m.

Your Telegram

Sir. E. Grey, to whom I communicated your telegram while suggesting how absolutely necessary it was for Your Excellency to give today some indication of British intentions, told me that at present he was not in a position to give me precise information on what he was going to say, as this was to be laid down in a Cabinet meeting this morning and might be modified according to the mood of the House of Commons. But he authorised me to inform you that you could state that he was making explanations to the Commons as to the present attitude of the British Government and that the chief of these declarations would be as follows:

'In case the German fleet came into the Channel or entered the North Sea in order to go round the British Isles with the object of attacking the French coasts or the French navy and of harassing French merchant shipping, the British fleet would intervene in order to give to French shipping its complete protection, in such a way that from that moment Great Britain and Germany would be in a state of war.'

Sir Edward Grey explained to me that the mention of an operation by way of the North Sea implied protection against a demonstration in the Atlantic Ocean.

On my return to the Embassy I received your telephonic communication relating to the German ultimatum addressed to Belgium. I immediately communicated to Sir Edward Grey.

Moltke to Jagow

Secret

Berlin, 4 August 1914

For the purpose of carrying through the war that has broken out, it is of the very greatest importance—an importance that cannot be over-emphasized—that the importation of foodstuffs into Germany through Italy remain unimpeded. Since Italy has not been willing to observe the obligations of her alliance, but has promised to observe a benevolent neutrality, the least she can do to prove this benevolence is to put no difficulties in our way in this connection.

I request that activities toward this end be undertaken at Rome at once. It is a question of life or death for us.

I request that the following be transmitted at once to London:

Germany wishes again to emphasize the fact that in her procedure in Belgium she was not guided by the intention of taking possession of Belgian territory on some frivolous pretext, even in the event of a hostile clash with Belgium. Germany's declaration to the Netherlands that she would not set foot on Dutch territory during the war, but, on the other hand, was determined to observe the strictest neutrality with regard to the Netherlands, is the best substantiation of the assurance just given. The English Government is able to see for itself that if Germany were cherishing any intention of acquiring Belgium territory, such an acquisition could only be of value if the same intention were being cherished toward Holland. It is here emphasized once again, that Germany's procedure in

Belgium was compelled, and could not help but be compelled, by the knowledge, acquired from reliable sources, of France's intended military operations. Germany could not afford to expose herself to the danger of attack by strong French forces in the direction of the Lower Rhine. Germany was forced to act on the principle that the offensive is the best defensive, which England, always ready to take the most energetic steps in time of war, should certainly understand better than anybody else. In this war it is a question for Germany, not only her whole national existence and of the continuation of the German Empire, created through so many bloody sacrifices, but also of the preservation and maintenance of German civilization and principles as against uncivilized Slavdom.

Germany is unable to believe that England will be willing to assist, by becoming an enemy of Germany, in destroying this civilization—civilization in which English spiritual culture has for ages had so large a share. This decision as to this lies in England's hands.

Note:

I would ask that this dispatch be sent to London uncoded, and that the Ambassador be advised to read it to Sir Edward Grey. It will not do us any harm if this note, by reason of its uncoded form, should also become known elsewhere.

Note to the Foreign Office: It is necessary continually to maintain toward the Belgian Government, even after the German invasion has taken place, the stand that Germany is ready at any moment to hold out to Belgium the hand of a brother, and is ever willing to enter upon negotiations concerning an acceptable *modus vivendi*, subject to the prosecution of the war forced upon us by France's procedure.

The indispensable basis of these negotiations, however, would have to remain the opening of Liege to the passage of German troops, and Belgium's assurance that she would not undertake the destruction of any railroads, bridges or artificial structures. Other demands than these would not be required from a military point of view.

Jagow to Lichnowsky
Telegram
> Berlin, 4 August 1914
> D. 10.20 a.m.

Please dispel any mistrust that may subsist on the part of British Government with regard to our intentions, by repeating most positively formal assurance that, even in the case of armed conflict with Belgium, Germany will, under no pretence whatever, annex Belgian territory. Sincerity of this declaration is borne out by fact that we solemnly pledged our word to Holland strictly to respect her neutrality. It is obvious that we could not profitably annex Belgian territory without making at the same time territorial acquisitions at expense of Holland. Please impress upon Sir E. Grey that German army could not be exposed to French attack across Belgium, which was planned according to absolutely unimpeachable information. Germany had consequently to disregard Belgian neutrality, it being for her a question of life or death to prevent French advance.

Lichnowsky to Jagow
Telegram 245

London, 4 August 1914

D. 10.02 a.m.

R. 1.37 p.m.

Yesterday I was not yet acquainted with the complete text of Sir E. Grey's speech, of which only a short parliamentary report was available. Since today's publication of its content in full, however, I must correct my impressions of yesterday by saying that I do not believe that we shall be able to count much longer on England's neutrality.

As I have repeatedly reported to Your Excellency, the question of the violation of Belgian neutrality constituted one of the most important factors in England's self-restraint. Mr. Asquith as well as Sir E. Grey had called this to my attention, and, as reported, I was able to convince myself before the session, that Sir E. Grey was in a state of intense excitement as the result of the violation of Belgian territory by our army.

What form British intervention will take, and whether it will take place at once, I am not able to judge. But I do not anticipate that, as I thought yesterday, from my knowledge gained only from extracts of the speech, the British Government will keep out, unless we are in a position to evacuate Belgian territory in the very shortest possible time. Hence we shall probably have to reckon on England's early hostility. The reception which met Sir E. Grey's speech in the House can be interpreted to mean that, outside of the left wing of its own party, the Government will have behind it the overwhelming majority of Parliament in any active policy the purpose of which is the protection of France and Belgium.

The news that reached here yesterday concerning the invasion of Belgium by German troops brought about a complete reversal of public opinion, to our disadvantage. The appeal of the King of the Belgians, made in moving language, has materially strengthened this impression.

Goschen to Grey
Telegram

Berlin, 4 August 1914

R. 13 August

Your telegram 266 of 4 August.

Secretary of State for Foreign Affairs regrets that he cannot give assurance demanded as German troops passed Belgian frontier this morning.

He begs me to assure you that this was military necessity and matter of life and death for Empire; every other line of attack would have taken too long and enabled Russia to concentrate. They had been ready to give, and had in fact given, assurances to Belgium that every compensation would be given to her after the war, and that her neutrality in every other way except as regards passage of troops would be respected. Belgium, he admitted, had acted quite naturally and very loyally in this matter.

Goschen to Grey
Telegram
> Berlin, 4 August 1914
> R. 13 August

Your telegram 270 of 4 August.

Both Chancellor and Secretary of State for Foreign Affairs regretted that they could give no other answer than that which they gave me this afternoon. I told them that in that case I had been instructed to ask for my passports.

My interview with the Chancellor was very painful. He said that he could not but consider it an intolerable thing that because they were taking the only course open to them to save the Empire from disaster, England should fall upon them just for the sake of the neutrality of Belgium. He looked upon England as entirely responsible for what might now happen.

I asked him whether he could not understand that we were bound in honour to do our best to preserve a neutrality which we had guaranteed. He said: 'But at what price!'

ACKNOWLEDGEMENTS

This book is historical narrative, rather than a work of primary research or scholarly interpretation. I have told stories of three historical figures. My aim has been to elucidate the theme of avoidable failure that seemed, to me, to link Custer, Thomas Andrews, and Edward Grey. My telling of these stories is informed by dozens of books (see the Bibliography) of research and interpretation as well as the stories of other authors writing for a lay audience. My greatest debt is to the scholars, researchers, and writers whose work has made my narrative possible.

I would like to thank those who encouraged me during the twelve-year period it took to write this book. I wish to particularly thank Patri Collins, the late Scott C. Davis, Fred Hunter, Zoe Landale, the late Cathryn Pisarski, and Dan Watkins.

BIBLIOGRAPHY

The Strange Ride of George Custer

Ambrose, Stephen E., *Crazy Horse and Custer: The Parallel Lives of Two American Warriors*, New York: Anchor Books, Doubleday, 1975.

Connell, Evan S., *Son of the Morning Star: Custer and the Little Bighorn*, New York: Harper & Row, 1984.

Custer, George A., *My Life on the Plains*, ed. Milo Milton Quaife, New York: The Citadel Press, 1962.

Graham, W.A., *The Custer Myth: A Source Book of Custeriana*, New York: Bonanza Books, 1953.

Gray, John S., *Centennial Campaign: The Sioux War of 1876*, Norman, Oklahoma and London: University of Oklahoma Press, 1988.

Karnow, Stanley, *Vietnam: A History*, New York: Penguin Books, 1997.

Monaghan, Jay, *Custer: The Life of General George Armstrong Custer*, Lincoln, Nebraska and London: University of Nebraska Press, 1959.

Sandoz, Mari, *The Battle of the Little Bighorn*, Lincoln, Nebraska and London: University of Nebraska Press, 1966.

Stewart, Edgar I, *Custer's Luck*, Norman, Oklahoma and London: University of Oklahoma Press, 1955.

Utley, Robert M., *Little Bighorn Battlefield*, Washington, D.C., Division of Publications National Park Service, 1988.

Welch, James and Stekler, Paul, *Killing Custer: The Battle of the Little Bighorn and the Fate of the Plains Indians*, New York Penguin Books, 1995.

Wooster, Robert, *The Military & United States: Indian Policy 1865-1903*, University of Nebraska Press, 1988.

The Short, Happy life of Thomas Andrews

Biel, Steven, *Down With The Old Canoe: A Cultural History of the Titanic Disaster*, New York & London; W.W. Norton Company, 1996.

Bullock, Shan F., *A Titanic Hero: Thomas Andrews, Shipbuilder*, Ludlow, Mass; 7C's Press, 1995.

Hardy, Thomas, *Hardy's Selected Poems*, New York; Dover Publications, Inc., 1995.

Janis, Irving L., *Victims of Groupthink: A Psychological Study Of Foreign-Policy Decisions and Fiascos*, Boston, Mass.; Houghton Mifflin Company, 1967.

Kuntz, Thomas ed., *The Titanic Hearings: The Official Transcripts of the 1912 Senate Investigations*, New York; Pocket Books,1998.

Langewiesche, William, *Inside the Sky: A Meditation on Flight*, New York; Pantheon Books, 1998.

Lord, Walter, *A Night To Remember*, Toronto, Ontario, Canada, New York, & London; Bantam Books, 1976.

Lord, Walter, *The Night Lives On*, New York; William Morrows Co., Inc, 1986.

Lynch, Don, *Titanic: An Illustrated History*, Toronto, Ontario, Canada; Madison Press Books, 1998.

Meredith, Lee W., *1912 Facts about Titanic*, Sunnydale, California; Historical Indexes, 1999.

The National Commission on Terrorist Attacks Upon the United States, *The 9/11 Commission Report*, New York; W.W. Norton & Company, 2004.

Pellegrino, Charles, *Her Name, Titanic: The Untold Story of the Sinking and Finding of The Unsinkable Ship*, New York; Avon Books, 1988.

Prange, Gordon W., *At Dawn We Slept: The Untold Story of Pearl Harbor*, New York; Penguin Books, 1991.

Vaughan, Diane, *The Challenger Launch Decision: Risky Technology, Culture, and Deviance at NASA*, Chicago & London; The University of Chicago Press, 1998.

Wade, Wyn Craig, *The Titanic: End of a Dream*, New York; Penguin Books, 1986.

Loss of the Steamship Titanic, Springfield, MA; 7C'S Press, 1912.

Titanic Disaster: Report of the Committee on Commerce United States Senate, Washington, D.C.; Government Printing Office, 1912.

The Story of the Titanic as Told by Its Survivors, Beesley, Lawrence, Bride, Harold, Gracie, Archibald, Lightoller, Commander, ed. Winocour, Jack, New York; Dover Publications, Inc., 1960.

The Last Man of the Nineteenth Century

Brook-Shepherd, Gordon, *Archduke of Sarajevo: The Romance and Tragedy of Franz Ferdinand of Austria;* Boston; Little Brown & Co., 1984.

Cassels, Lavender, *The Archduke and the Assassin: Sarajevo, June 28th 1914*; New York; Dorset Press, 1988.

Churchill, Winston S., *The World Crisis*, New York; Charles Scribner's Sons, 1931.

Fussell, Paul, *The Great War and Modern Memory*, New York; Oxford University Press, 1975.

Geiss, Imanuel, ed., *July 1914: The Outbreak of the First World War*, New York; W. W. Norton & Company Inc, 1967.

Gilbert, Martin, *The First World War: A Complete History*, New York; Henry Holt and Company, 1994.

Grey, Sir Edward, *Twenty-Five Years 1892-1916 Volumes I & II*, New York; Frederick A. Stockes Co., 1925.

Hemingway, Ernest, *A Farewell to Arms*, New York; Scribner's Paperback Fiction, 1995.

Keegan, John, *A History of Warfare*, New York; Vintage Books, 1993.

Massie, Robert K., *Dreadnought: Britain, Germany, and the Coming of the Great War*, New York; Random House, 1991.

Robbins, Keith, *Sir Edward Grey: A Biography of Lord Grey of Fallodon*, London; Cassell, 1971.

Stevens, Wallace, *The Collected Poems of Wallace Stevens*, New York, Alfred Knopf, 1981.

Taylor, Edmond, *The Fall of the Dynasties: The Collapse of the Old Order 1905-1922*, Ed. John Gunther, New York; Doubleday & Company, Inc. 1963.

Trevelyan, G. M., *Grey of Fallodon*, New York; Longmans Green, 1937.

Tuchman, Barbara, *The Guns of August*, New York; Dell Publishing Co., 1962.

Tuchman, Barbara, *Practicing History*, New York; Ballantine Books, 1981.

Index

CUNE PRESS WAS FOUNDED in 1994 to publish thoughtful writing of public importance. Our name is derived from "cuneiform." (In Latin *cuni* means "wedge.")

In the ancient Near East the development of cuneiform script—simpler and more adaptable than hieroglyphics—enabled a large class of merchants and landowners to become literate. Clay tablets inscribed with wedge-shaped stylus marks made possible a broad inter-meshing of individual efforts in trade and commerce.

Cuneiform enabled scholarship to exist, art to flower, and created what historians define as the world's first civilization. When the Phoenicians developed their sound-based alphabet, they expressed it in cuneiform.

The idea of Cune Press is the democratization of learning, the faith that rarefied ideas—pulled from dusty pedestals and displayed in the streets—can transform the lives of ordinary people. And it is the conviction that ordinary people, trusted with the most precious gifts of civilization, will give our culture elasticity and depth—a necessity if we are to survive in a time of rapid change.

Aswat: Voices from a Small Planet (a series from Cune Press)

Looking Both Ways	Pauline Kaldas
Stage Warriors	Sarah Imes Borden
Stories My Father Told Me	Helen Zughraib

 Syria Crossroads (a series from Cune Press)

Leaving Syria	Bill Dienst & Madi Williamson
Visit the Old City of Aleppo	Khaldoun Fansa
The Dusk Visitor	Musa Al-Halool
Steel & Silk	Sami Moubayed
Syria - A Decade of Lost Chances	Carsten Wieland
The Road from Damascus	Scott C. Davis
A Pen of Damascus Steel	Ali Ferzat
White Carnations	Musa Rahum Abbas

 Bridge Between the Cultures (a series from Cune Press)

Finding Melody Sullivan	Alice Rothchild
Escape to Aswan	Amal Sedky Winter
Confessions of a Knight Errant	Gretchen McCullough
Afghanistan & Beyond	Linda Sartor
Apartheid is a Crime	Mats Svensson
The Passionate Spies	John Harte
Congo Prophet	Frederic Hunter
Music Has No Boundaries	Rafique Gangat
Muslims, Arabs & Arab Americans	Nawar Shora

 Cune Cune Press: www.cunepress.com

STEVEN SCHLESSER IS AN INDEPENDENT SCHOLAR and freelance writer based in Portland, Oregon. A graduate of Claremont McKenna College and Vermont Law School, Schlesser served his apprenticeship as a journalist for the *Valley Herald of Milton-Freewater* and the *Walla Walla Union-Bulletin*. He currently works in the wood products industry and writes a monthly newsletter called *The Schlesser Review*.

Schlesser has a long-standing love of British culture and history, particularly the Edwardian and Victorian eras. His primary current interest, however, is work on a teacher's guide to George Orwell.

For more information, please write us at stevenschlesser@gmail.com.

Printed in the USA
CPSIA information can be obtained
at www.ICGtesting.com
JSHW011353161023
50269JS00018B/125